KEY CASES

CONTRACT LAW

CHRIS TURNER

Hodder Arnold

A MEMBER OF THE

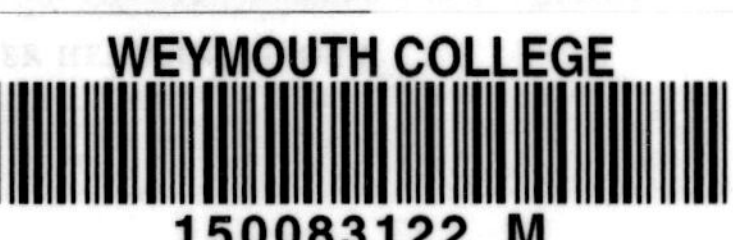

Orders: please contact Bookpoint Ltd, 130 Milton Park, Abingdon, Oxon OX14 4SB. Telephone: (44) 01235 827720. Fax: (44) 01235 400454. Lines are open from 9.00 – 6.00, Monday to Saturday, with a 24 hour message answering service. You can also order through our website www.hoddereducation.co.uk

If you have any comments to make about this, or any of our other titles, please send them to educationenquiries@hodder.co.uk

British Library Cataloguing in Publication Data
A catalogue record for this title is available from the British Library

ISBN-10: 0 340 91500 5
ISBN-13: 978 0 340 91500 4

This edition published 2006
Impression number 10 9 8 7 6 5 4 3 2 1
Year 2009 2008 2007 2006

Hodder Headline's policy is to use papers that are natural, renewable and recyclable products and made from wood grown in sustainable forests. The logging and manufacturing processes are expected to conform to the environmental regulations of the country of origin.

Typeset by Transet Limited, Coventry, England.
Printed in Great Britain for Hodder Arnold, an imprint of Hodder Education, a member of the Hodder Headline Group, 338 Euston Road, London NW1 3BH by Cox & Wyman Ltd., Reading, Berkshire.

CONTENTS

TABLE OF CASES v

PREFACE xi

Chapter 1 FORMATION OF A CONTRACT

1.1 Offer 2
1.2 Acceptance 9
1.3 Consideration 17
1.4 Intention to create legal relations 28

Chapter 2 CAPACITY

2.1 Corporations and capacity 35
2.2 Capacity and minors' contracts 37

Chapter 3 THIRD PARTY RIGHTS AND PRIVITY OF CONTRACT

3.1 The basic rule and its effects 41
3.2 Exceptions to the strict rule 42

Chapter 4 THE CONTENTS OF A CONTRACT

4.1 Representations 50
4.2 Terms 51
4.3 Judicial and statutory control of exclusion clauses 63

Chapter 5 VITIATING FACTORS

5.1 Misrepresentation 74
5.2 Mistake 81
5.3 Duress, economic duress and undue influence 89
5.4 Illegality 100

Chapter 6 DISCHARGE OF A CONTRACT

6.1 Discharge by performance 111
6.2 Discharge by agreement 113
6.3 Discharge by frustration 114
6.4 Discharge by breach 122

Chapter 7 REMEDIES

7.1 Unliquidated damages 126
7.2 Liquidated damage clauses 132
7.3 Claims for *quantum meruit* 132
7.4 Equitable remedies 133

Index **137**

TABLE OF CASES

Adams v Lindsell [1818] 106 ER 250 ....1, 14
Affreteurs Reunis SA v Walford (Walford's case) [1919] AC 801 ....41, 42
Ailsa Craig Fishing Co Ltd v Malvern Fishing Co Ltd [1983] 1 WLR 964 ....49, 68
Alfred McAlpine Construction Ltd v Panatown Ltd (1998) 88 BLR 67........44
Allcard v Skinner (1887) 36 Ch D 45 ....73, 93
Amalgamated Investment & Property Co Ltd v John Walker & Sons Ltd [1977] 1 WLR 164 118
Ashbury Railway Carriage Co Ltd v Riche (1875) LR 7 HL 653 35
Associated Provincial Picture House v Wednesbury Corporation [1948] 1 KB 223 57
Atlas Express Ltd v Kafco (Importers and Distributors) Ltd [1989] QB 833 ....73, 91, 92
Attorney-General v Blake [2001] 1 AC 268 ....125, 129
Attwood v Lamont [1920] 3 KB 571....................73, 106
Avery v Bowden (1855) 5 E & B 714 ....110, 123

Balfour v Balfour [1919] 2 KB 571 ....1, 28, 30
Bank of Credit and Commerce International SA v Aboody [1990] 1 QB 923....................94
Barclays Bank plc v Boulter and Another [1997] 2 All ER 1002....................99
Barclays Bank plc v O'Brien [1993] 4 All ER 417 ....95, 97, 99
Barton v Armstrong [1975] 2 All ER 465 ....73, 89
Bell v Lever Brothers Ltd [1932] AC 161 ....73, 82
Beswick v Beswick [1968] AC 58....................41, 47
Bettini v Gye (1876) 1 QBD 183 ....49, 60
Bissett v Wilkinson [1927] AC 177 ....49, 50
Bolton v Mahadeva [1972] 1 WLR 1009 112
Brinkibon v Stahag Stahl [1983] AC 34....................16
British Petroleum Exploration Co (Libya) Ltd v Hunt (No 2) [1979] 1 WLR 783 ....110, 121
British Russian Gazette Ltd v Associated Newspapers Ltd [1933] 2 KB 616....................110, 113
British Steel Corporation v Cleveland Bridge and Engineering Co [1984] 1 All ER 504 12
British Westinghouse Electric and Manufacturing Co Ltd v Underground Electric Railways Co of London Ltd [1912] AC 673....................125, 130
Brogden v Metropolitan Railway Co (1877) 2 App Cas 666....................11
Bunge Corporation v Tradax Export SA [1981] 1 WLR 711 ....110, 122

Butler Machine Tool Co Ltd v Ex-Cell-O Corporation [1979] 1 WLR 401 13

Candler v Crane, Christmas & Co [1951] 2 KB 164 77
Carlill v The Carbolic Smoke Ball Co Ltd [1893] 1 QB 256 ....1, 4
Casey's Patent, *Re* [1892] 1 Ch 104....1, 21
Cehave NV v Bremer Handelsgesselschaft mbH, *The Hansa Nord* [1976] QB 44 61
Central London Property Trust Ltd v High Trees House Ltd [1947] KB 130 ....1, 26
Chandler v Webster [1904] 1 KB 493....116, 119
Chapelton v Barry Urban District Council [1940] 1 KB 532 64
Chappell v Nestlé [1960] AC 87 ....1, 18
Chapple v Cooper (1844) 3 M & W 252 37
Cheese v Thomas [1994] 1 All ER 35 99
Clarke v Dickson [1858] 120 ER 463 ....125, 135
Clements v London and North Western Railway Company [1894] 2 QB 482....38
Combe v Combe [1951] 2 KB 215 27
Cooper v Phibbs (1867) LR 3 HL 149 81
Cope v Rowlands (1836) 2 M & W 149....73, 100
Couturier v Hastie (1852) 5 HLC 673 ....73, 81
Craddock Bros Ltd v Hunt [1923] 2 Ch 136 ....125, 136
Cundy v Lindsay (1878) 3 App Cas 459 ....73, 85
Currie v Misa (1875) 1 App Cas 554....17
Curtis v Chemical Cleaning and Dyeing Co Ltd [1951] 1 KB 805 ....49, 66
Cutter v Powell (1795) 6 Term Rep 320....110, 111

D & C Builders v Rees [1965] 3 All ER 837....26
Davis Contractors Ltd v Fareham Urban District Council [1956] AC 696 ....110, 118
De Francesco v Barnum (1890) 45 Ch D 430 ....35, 38
Denny, Mott & Dickson Ltd v James B Fraser & Co Ltd [1944] 1 All ER 678 ....110, 116
Derry v Peek (1889) 14 App Cas 337 ....73, 76
Dickinson v Dodds (1876) 2 Ch D 463 ....1, 8
Director General of Fair Trading v First National Bank plc [2002] 1 All ER 97 ....49, 72
Dunlop v Lambert (1839) 6 Cl & F 600....44
Dunlop Pneumatic Tyre Co v New Garage and Motor Co [1914] AC 79 ....125, 132
Dunlop Pneumatic Tyre Co v Selfridge & Co [1915] AC 847 ....1, 17, 41, 42

Eastham v Newcastle United Football Club Ltd [1964] Ch 413....103
Edgington v Fitzmaurice (1885) 29 Ch D 459 ....73, 74
Edwards v Skyways Ltd [1969] 1 WLR 349 ....1, 31
Entores Ltd v Miles Far East Corporation [1955] 2 QB 327 ....1, 15
Errington v Errington & Woods [1952] 1 KB 290 ....1, 8

Esso Petroleum Co Ltd v Commissioners of Customs and Excise
[1976] 1 All ER 117 32
Esso Petroleum Co Ltd v Harper's Garage (Stourport) Ltd
[1968] AC 269, HL 104
Esso Petroleum Co Ltd v Marden [1976] QB 801 50
Evans (J) & Son (Portsmouth) Ltd v Andrea Merzario Ltd [1976]
1 WLR 1078 53

Faccenda Chicken v Fowler [1986] 1 All ER 617 134
Farley v Skinner [2001] 3 WLR 899, HL 125, 128
Fellowes v Fisher [1976] QB 122 133
Felthouse v Bindley [1863] 142 ER 1037 ....1, 13
Fibrosa Spolka Akcyjna v Fairbairn Lawson Combe Barbour Ltd
(The Fibrosa Case) [1943] AC 32 ....110, 120
Fisher v Bell [1961] 1 QB 394 ....1, 2
Fitch v Dewes [1921] 2 AC 158 102
Fletcher v Krell (1873) 42 LJ QB 55 81
Foakes v Beer (1884) 9 App Cas 605 ....26, 28

George Mitchell Ltd v Finney Lock Seeds Ltd [1983] 2 AC 803 70
Glassbrook Bros v Glamorgan County Council [1925] AC 270 23
Godley v Perry [1960] 1 WLR 9, QBD 59
Goldsoll v Goldman [1915] 1 Ch 292 107
Grant v Australian Knitting Mills [1936] AC 85 ....49, 59
Great Peace Shipping Ltd v Tsavliris Salvage (International) Ltd [2002]
EWCA Civ 1407 ....83, 88
Green v Russell [1959] 2 QB 226 43
Guthing v Lynn (1831) 2 B & Ad 232 7

Hadley v Baxendale (1854) 9 Exch 341 ....125, 126, 127
Hall v Woolston Hall Leisure Ltd [2000] 4 All ER 787 108
Hanover Insurance Brokers Ltd and Christchurch Insurance Brokers Ltd
v Schapiro [1994] IRLR 82 101
Harris v Nickerson (1873) LR 8 QB 286 3
Hartley v Ponsonby (1857) 7 E & B 872 23
Harvela Investments Ltd v Royal Trust Co. of Canada Ltd [1986] AC 207 6
Harvey v Facey [1893] AC 552 4
Hedley Byrne & Co Ltd v Heller & Partners Ltd [1964] AC 465 ....73, 77, 78
Herbert Morris Ltd v Saxelby [1916] 1 AC 688, HL 73, 101
Herne Bay Steamboat Co v Hutton [1903] 2 KB 683 117
Hochster v De la Tour (1853) 2 E & B 678 ....110, 122
Hoenig v Isaacs [1952] 2 All ER 176 ....110, 112
Hollier v Rambler Motors (AMC) Ltd [1972] QB 71 ....49, 67
Home Counties Dairies Ltd v Skilton [1970] 1 WLR 526 102
Hong Kong Fir Shipping Co Ltd v Kawasaki Kisen Kaisha Ltd [1962]
2 QB 26 62
Household Fire Insurance v Grant (1879) 4 Ex D 216 15
Howard Marine Dredging Co Ltd v A Ogden & Sons (Excavating) Ltd
[1978] QB 574 ....73, 78

Hutton v Warren [1836] 150 ER 517 54
Hyde v Wrench [1840] 49 ER 132 ....1, 9

Jackson v Horizon Holidays [1975] 1 WLR 1468 ....125, 131
Jackson v Union Marine Insurance Ltd (1874) LR 10 CP 125....................119
Jarvis v Swan Tours Ltd [1973] 1 QB 23 131
Jones v Padavatton [1969] 1 WLR 328 31

Kendall (Henry) & Sons v William Lillico & Sons Ltd [1969] 2 AC 31 58
Kings Norton Metal Co Ltd v Edridge, Merrett & Co Ltd
(The Kings Norton Metal Case) (1897) 14 TLR 98 ....85, 86
Kleinwort Benson Ltd v Malaysian Mining Corporation [1989]
1 WLR 379 34
Krell v Henry [1903] 2 KB 740....................110, 116, 119

Lampleigh v Braithwaite [1615] 80 ER 255 ....21, 24
Leslie (R) Ltd v Sheill [1914] 3 KB 607 ....35, 39
L'Estrange v Graucob [1934] 2 KB 394 ....49, 52
Lewis v Avery [1972] 1 QB 198....................73, 86
Liverpool City Council v Irwin [1976] 2 WLR 562 ....49, 56
Locker and Woolf Ltd v Western Australian Insurance Co Ltd [1936]
1 KB 408 80
London Joint Stock Bank v MacMillan [1918] AC 777 ....125, 126
Long v Lloyd [1958] 1 WLR 753 ....125, 135

McArdle, *Re* [1951] Ch 669....................1, 20
McCutcheon v MacBrayne Ltd [1964] 1 WLR 125 ....49, 63
Maritime National Fish Ltd v Ocean Trawlers Ltd [1935] AC 524 ....110, 117
Merritt v Merritt [1970] 1 WLR 1211 ....1, 29
Moorcock, The (1889) 14 PD 64 ....49, 55
Moore & Co and Landauer & Co's Arbitration, Re [1921] 2 KB 519..........58
Morgan v Manser [1948] 1 QB 184 115
Museprime Properties Ltd v Adhill Properties Ltd [1990] EGLR 196 75

Napier v The National Business Agency [1951] 2 All ER 264 105
Nash v Inman [1908] 2 KB 1 ....35, 37
National Westminster Bank v Morgan [1985] AC 686....................73, 93
New Zealand Shipping Co Ltd v AM Satterthwaite & Co Ltd,
The Eurymedon [1975] AC 154 ....13, 45
Nordenfelt v Maxim Nordenfelt Co [1894] AC 535 ....73, 103
North Ocean Shipping Co Ltd v Hyundai Construction Co Ltd,
The Atlantic Baron [1978] QB 705 92

Occidental Worldwide Investment Corporation v Skibs A/S Avanti,
The Siboen, The Sibotre [1976] 1 Lloyd's Rep 293 90
Olley v Marlborough Court Hotels [1949] 1 KB 532....................49, 63
Oscar Chess Ltd v Williams [1957] 1 WLR 370....................49, 51
Overland Shoes Ltd v Shenkers Ltd [1998] 1 Lloyd's Rep 498....................71

Page One Records v Britton [1968] 1 WLR 157 ....125, 134
Panayiotou v Sony Music International (UK) Ltd [1994] 1 All ER 755....104
Pao On v Lau Yiu Long [1980] AC 614 23
Paradine v Jane (1647) Aleyn 26 ....110, 114
Paragon Finance v Nash [2001] EWCA Civ 1466 57
Parker v Clarke [1960] 1 WLR 286....30
Parker v South Eastern Railway Co (1877) 2 CPD 416 65
Parkinson v College of Ambulance Ltd and Harrison [1925] 2 KB 1....73, 106
Pars Technology Ltd v City Link Transport Holdings Ltd [1999] EWCA Civ 1822....11
Parsons (H) (Livestock) Ltd v Uttley Ingham [1978] QB 791 128
Partridge v Crittenden [1968] 1 WLR 1204 3
Pearce v Brooks (1866) LR 1 Ex 213....73, 106
Peyman v Lanjani [1985] 2 WLR 154....74
Pharmaceutical Society of Great Britain v Boots Cash Chemists Ltd [1953] 1 All ER 482 2
Photo Productions Ltd v Securicor Transport Ltd [1980] AC 827 67
Pinnel's Case (1602) 5 Co Rep 117a 27
Planche v Colburn (1831) 8 Bing 14....110, 112
Posner v Scott-Lewis [1987] Ch 25 133
Poussard v Spiers and Pond (1876) 1 QBD 410 ....49, 60
Price v Easton [1833] 110 ER 518....41

Raffles v Wichelhaus [1864] 159 ER 375 ....73, 84
Ramsgate Victoria Hotel Co. Ltd v Montefiore (1866) Lr 1 Ex 109....9
Reardon Smith Line v Hansen-Tangen [1976] 1 WLR 989 ....49, 62
Redgrave v Hurd (1881) 20 Ch D 1 ....73, 80
Rolled Steel Products (Holdings) Ltd v British Steel Corporation [1985] 2 WLR 908 ....35, 36
Roscorla v Thomas [1842] 3 QB 234 21
Rose and Frank Co v J R Crompton & Bros [1923] 2 KB 261; [1925] AC 445 ....1, 33
Routledge v Grant (1828) 4 Bing 653 7
Routledge v McKay [1954] 1 WLR 615 52
Rowland v Divall [1923] 2 KB 500 57
Royal Bank of Scotland plc v Etridge (No 2) and other appeals [2001] UKHL 44 ....73, 96
Royscot Trust Ltd v Rogerson [1991] 3 All ER 294 79
Ruxley Electronics and Construction Ltd v Forsyth; Laddingford Enclosures Ltd v Forsyth [1995] 3 All ER 268, HL....129, 131
Ryan v Mutual Tontine Westminster Chambers Association [1893] 1 Ch 116....125, 133

Saunders v Anglian Building Society [1970] AC 1004 88
Schawel v Reade [1913] 2 IR 64 54
Schuler (L) AG v Wickman Machine Tool Sales Ltd [1974] AC 235 ....49, 61
Selectmove, *Re* [1995] 2 All ER 531 28
Shanklin Pier v Detel Products Ltd [1951] 2 KB 854....41, 46
Shell (UK) Ltd v Lostock Garages Ltd [1977] 1 All ER 481....49, 55

Shogun Finance Ltd v Hudson [2003] UKHL 62 87
Simpkins v Pays [1955] 1 WLR 975 30
Smith v Hughes (1871) LR 6 QB 597 84
Smith New Court Securities v Scrimgeour Vickers [1996] 4 All ER 769 76
Snelling v John G Snelling Ltd [1973] 1 QB 87 45
Solle v Butcher [1950] 1 KB 671 87
Spice Girls Ltd v Aprilia World Service BV [2000] EMLR 478 75
Spurling (L) Ltd v Bradshaw [1956] 1 WLR 561 ....64, 66
Startup v Macdonald (1843) 6 Man & G 593 113
Steinberg v Scala (Leeds) Ltd [1923] 2 Ch 452 ....35, 39
Stevenson v McLean (1880) 5 QBD 346 10
Stilk v Myrick [1809] 170 ER 1168 ....1, 20, 22, 25, 26
Sumpter v Hedges [1898] 1 QB 673 ....110, 111

Taddy v Sterious [1904] 1 Ch 354 44
Taylor v Caldwell (1863) 32 LJ QB 164 ....110, 114
Taylor v Laird (1856) 25 LJ Ex 329 6
Thomas v Thomas [1842] 2 QB 851 18
Thornton v Shoe Lane Parking Ltd [1971] 2 QB 163 ....49, 65
Tinsley v Milligan [1993] 3 WLR 126 108
Tulk v Moxhay [1848] 41 ER 1143 43
Tweddle v Atkinson [1861] 121 ER 762 ....1, 21

Upton Rural District Council v Powell [1942] 1 All ER 220 ....125, 132

Victoria Laundry Ltd v Newman Industries Ltd [1949] 2 KB 528 127

Ward v Byham [1956] 1 WLR 496 19
Watford Electronics Ltd v Sanderson CFL [2001] 1 All ER (Comm) 696 ....49, 70
Webster v Cecil [1861] 54 ER 812 88
Wednesbury Principle, *see* Associated Provincial Picture House v Wednesbury Corporation
White v Bluett (1853) 23 LJ Ex 36 19
White and Carter Ltd v McGregor [1962] AC 413 124
Williams v Bayley (1886) LR 1 HL 200 89
Williams v Roffey Bros & Nicholls Contractors Ltd [1990] 1 All ER 512 ....1, 25, 28
Woodar Investment Development Ltd v Wimpey Construction UK Ltd [1980] 1 All ER 571 131

PREFACE

The Key Cases series is designed to give a clear understanding of important cases. This is useful when studying a new topic and invaluable as a revision aid.

Each case is broken down into fact and law. In addition, many cases are extended by the use of important extracts from the judgment or by comment or by highlighting problems. In some instances students are reminded that there is a link to other cases or material. The Key Link symbol alerts readers to links within the book and also to cases and other material especially statutory provisions which are not included in the book.

To create a clear layout, symbols have been used at the start of each component of the case. The symbols are:

Key Facts – These are the basic facts of the case.

Key Law – This is the major principle of law in the case, the *ratio decidendi.*

Key Judgment – This is an actual extract from a judgment made on the case.

Key Comment – Influential or appropriate comments made on the case.

Key Problem – Apparent inconsistencies or difficulties in the law.

Key Link – This indicates other cases in the text which should be considered with this case.

At the start of each chapter there are mind maps highlighting the main cases and points of law. Also, in most chapters, one or two of the most important cases are boxed to identify them and stress their importance.

Each Key Cases book can be used in conjunction with the Key Facts book on the same subject. Equally they can be used as additional material to support any other textbook.

The Key Cases book on Contract Law starts with cases on formation and then covers the main cases on capacity, privity of contract, terms and exclusion clauses, the vitiating factors, discharge of a contract and remedies for breach of contract.

The law is as I believe it to be at 1st December 2005.

Chris Turner

CHAPTER 1

FORMATION OF A CONTRACT

Offer and acceptance:
An offer must be distinguished from an invitation to treat which is an invitation to the other party to make an offer to buy *Fisher v Bell*
An offer must be communicated but can be made to the whole world or to an individual *Carlill v The Carbolic Smoke Ball Co. Ltd*
An offer can be withdrawn any time up to acceptance and this can be through a reliable third party *Dickinson v Dodds*
In unilateral offers acceptance is done through performance and the offer cannot be withdrawn while performance is under way *Errington v Errington & Woods*
Acceptance must be unconditional and a counter offer means the offer is no longer open to accept *Hyde v Wrench*
Silence can never be acceptance *Felthouse v Bindley*
Where the use of the postal system is the normal anticipated mode of acceptance the acceptance occurs when the letter is posted, not when it is received *Adams v Lindsell*
Modern communication methods present other problems *Entores Ltd v Miles Far East Corporation*

Formation

Consideration:
Consideration is the price for which the promise of the other is bought *Dunlop Pneumatic Tyre Co. v Selfridge & Co.*
Consideration must be real, tangible and of value *Chappell v Nestlé*
Past consideration is no consideration *Re McArdle*
Unless there is an implied promise to pay *Re Casey's Patent*
Consideration must move from the promisee *Tweddle v Atkinson*
Performance of an existing obligation can never be consideration for a fresh promise *Stilk v Myrick*
Unless something extra is given or an extra benefit is gained *Williams v Roffey Bros & Nicholls Contractors Ltd*
Where a party agrees to waive existing rights under a contract and the other party acts in reasonable reliance the party making the promise is prevented from going back on it *Central London Property Trust Ltd v High Trees House Ltd*

Intention to create legal relations:
Domestic arrangements are presumed not to give rise to legal relations *Balfour v Balfour*
Unless the contrary is proved *Merritt v Merritt*
Business arrangements are presumed to lead to legal relations *Edwards v Skyways Ltd*
Unless a contrary intent can be shown *Rose and Frank Co v J R Crompton & Bros*

1.1 Offer

1.1.1 The character of an offer

CA ***Phrmaceutical Society of GB v Boots Cash Chemists Ltd*** **[1953] 1 All ER 482**

Boots refurbished a shop into a self-service system which at the time was novel. By s 18 Pharmacy and Poisons Act 1933 the sale of certain drugs and poisons should not occur except 'under the supervision of a registered pharmacist'. The point at which the contract was formed was therefore critical, either when the customer removed goods from the shelves or when they were presented to the cash desk for payment.

The court held that the contract was formed when goods were presented at the cash desk where a pharmacist was present, not when taken from the shelf. Mere display of the goods on the shelves was an invitation to treat.

Somervell LJ identified that 'one of the most formidable difficulties in the way of the plaintiff's contention [is that] once an article has been placed in the receptacle the customer himself is bound and would have no right, without paying for the first article, to substitute an article which he saw later and ... preferred'.

Fisher v Bell **[1961] 1 QB 394**

The Offensive Weapons Act 1959 prohibited 'offering for sale' various offensive weapons including flick knives. A shopkeeper displayed some in his window and was prosecuted unsuccessfully.

The court held that this display of the weapon was not offering the prohibited weapon for sale but was a mere invitation to treat, an invitation to the customer to make an offer to buy.

DC ***Partridge v Crittenden*** **[1968] 1 WLR 1204**

The defendant was prosecuted under the Protection of Birds Act 1954 for 'offering for sale' a wild bird. He had advertised 'Bramblefinch cocks, bramblefinch hens, 25s each'. The Divisional Court quashed his conviction.

The court held that the advertisement was not an offer but an invitation to treat. It was the starting point of negotiations with anyone reading it and responding to it.

QB ***Harris v Nickerson*** **(1873) LR 8 QB 286**

The claimant attended an auction hoping to buy some furniture that was advertised in the auction catalogue. The auctioneer withdrew the items from sale and the claimant sued unsuccessfully for the cost of travel and lodgings.

The court held that the presence of the goods in the catalogue was no more than an invitation to treat, and that there was no contract since this could only be formed on fall of the auctioneer's hammer.

There is an absolute entitlement to withdraw any lot prior to the fall of the auctioneer's hammer, an example of the rule that an offer can be withdrawn any time prior to acceptance.

PC ***Harvey v Facey* [1893] AC 552**

Harvey wanted to buy Facey's farm and sent a telegram 'Will you sell me Bumper Hall? Telegraph lowest price'. Facey's telegram replied 'Lowest price acceptable £900'. Harvey argued that he had then accepted this and sued when the farm was sold to another person. His action failed.

The court held that the statement was merely a statement of price and was not an offer open to acceptance.

CA ***Carlill v The Carbolic Smoke Ball Co. Ltd* [1893] 1 QB 256**

The company advertised the smoke ball, a patent medicine, and promised that any purchaser using it correctly would be immune from a range of illnesses including influenza. The company also stated in the advertisement that anyone using the product who still got flu would receive £100. Mrs Carlill did get flu after using the smoke ball in the fashion stated and sued successfully for the £100.

The company raised numerous defences, that the advertisement was a mere puff; that there was no offer made to a specific person; that there was no notification of acceptance, but all were rejected.

The court held that the company made an offer to the whole world which was accepted by buying the smoke ball, using it and still getting flu. It was a unilateral offer and, unlike bilateral contracts where offer and acceptance are both stated, performance and acceptance were the same. The situation was no different to any where a reward is offered. Advertisements are normally seen as only invitations to treat, with the hope that persons reading them are persuaded to offer to purchase the product after which a contract is formed. However, the precise wording was held to indicate a contractual relationship quite separate to the contract for the sale and purchase of the smoke ball. The court enforced the claim for the £100. The promise was an offer open to acceptance by anyone who used the smoke ball correctly and still got flu. The company was contractually bound by the offer to pay the sum.

Lindley LJ said 'it is said that [the offer] is not made to anyone in particular. Now that point is common to the words of this advertisement and to the words of all other advertisements offering rewards. They are offers to anyone who performs the conditions named in the advertisement, and anybody who does perform the condition accepts the offer'. **Bowen LJ** said. 'The advertisement says that £1,000 is lodged at the bank for that purpose. Therefore it cannot be said that the statement that £100 would be paid was intended to be a mere puff. I think it was intended to be understood by the public as an offer which was to be acted upon'.

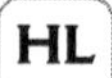

Harvela Investments Ltd v Royal Trust Co. of Canada Ltd **[1986] AC 207**

The Trust company wished to sell land in a single transaction and had invited tenders from two interested parties. They indicated to both prospective purchasers that the sale would go to the party making the highest bid. The party making the lowest bid tendered a price of $2,100,000 but included an alternative bid of $101,000 in excess of any other offer (a referential bid). The company accepted this referential bid and Harvela, the party that had made the higher bid, discovered this and sued the Trust company successfully.

The court had to decide if the invitation to tender was, as would usually be the case, only an invitation to treat and which bid was the higher. It held that the wording of the invitation to tender made it an offer that could only be accepted by the highest bidder, and that the referential bid could not be accepted as binding in law. If both parties entered such a bid then no contract could emerge since each referential bid in turn would be higher than the other which in turn would invoke the other referential bid and so the contract could never be complete. It could not accept the referential bid as valid.

1.1.2 Communication of offers

Exch ***Taylor v Laird*** **(1856) 25 LJ Ex 329**

The claimant captained the defendant's ship but then decided to give up the captaincy but worked his passage back home as a crew member. He then tried to claim wages but failed.

The court held that, since the ship owner was unaware of the claimant's decision to quit as captain and had received no offer to work in an alternative capacity, there was no contract. A person can only accept an offer that has been communicated to him.

KB **_Guthing v Lynn_ (1831) 2 B & Ad 232**

In a contract for the sale and purchase of a horse the defendant promised to pay an additional £5 ' if the horse is lucky'.

The court held that the promise was not enforceable since it was too vague. There was no way for the court to decide what 'lucky' meant so the defendant could not be bound by the promise.

1.1.3 Revocation of offers

CP **_Routledge v Grant_ (1828) 4 Bing 653**

The defendant offered his house for sale, the offer to remain open for six weeks only. He then took the house off the market before this period ended and was sued.

The court held that withdrawal of an offer is lawful any time up to acceptance. Since there had been no acceptance he acted lawfully.

Dickinson v Dodds (1876) 2 Ch D 463

Dodds offered to sell houses to Dickinson, the offer to remain open until 9.00 am on 12th June. Dickinson intended to accept the offer but did not do so at once. Berry, a mutual acquaintance, then told Dickinson that Dodds had withdrawn the offer and Dickinson sent an acceptance, but when it was received the house was already sold. Dickinson claimed unlawful revocation and breach of contract.

The court held that revocation must be communicated any time before acceptance but this can be through a reliable third party – as Berry was shown to be. The offer was validly withdrawn.

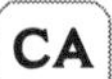

Errington v Errington & Woods [1952] 1 KB 290

A father bought and mortgaged a house in his own name for his son and daughter-in-law to live in, promising that, when they had paid off the mortgage, he would transfer legal title to them. The father later died and other family members sought possession but failed.

The court held that the father's promise could not be withdrawn while the couple kept up the mortgage repayments, after which the house would be legally theirs. There was a unilateral contract where acceptance and performance were one and the same.

Lord Denning explained 'the father's promise was a unilateral contract ... the house in return for ... paying the instalments. It could not be revoked ... once the couple entered on performance ... but it would cease to bind him if they left it incomplete and unperformed, which they have not done' (the '*Errington* principle').

This is the same principle that applies to rewards.

1.1.4 Termination of offers

Exch **_Ramsgate Victoria Hotel Co. Ltd v Montefiore_**
(1866) LR 1 Ex 109

The defendant offered to buy shares in June but shares were not issued till November. He refused to pay and the claimant sued.

It was held that the offer to buy had lapsed. It would be unreasonable for an offer to stay open indefinitely, only for a reasonable time which had passed here.

1.2 Acceptance

1.2.1 The basic rules of acceptance

RC **_Hyde v Wrench_ [1840] 49 ER 132**

The defendant offered to sell his farm to the claimant for

£1,000 who instead offered the lower price of £950. When the defendant rejected this price the defendant tried to accept the original price and claimed breach of contract when the sale did not occur.

The court held that the counter was a rejection of the original offer, meaning that it was no longer open to acceptance.

Lord Langdale said 'if [the offer] had at once been unconditionally accepted, there would … have been a … binding contract; instead … the plaintiff made an offer of his own … and he thereby rejected the offer previously made … it was not afterwards competent for him to revive the proposal … by tendering an acceptance of it; … therefore, there exists no obligation of any sort between the parties'.

QB ***Stevenson v McLean*** **(1880) 5 QBD 346**

The defendant offered to sell iron to the claimant, who in his reply wanted to know if delivery could be staggered over two months. On receiving no reply the claimant then sent a letter of acceptance and sued successfully when the iron was sold to another party.

The court held that the claimant's initial response was not a counter offer and thus a rejection of the offer; it was merely an enquiry about details, so that the offer was still open to acceptance. The claimant had done this and so a contract was formed which was breached.

Pars Technology Ltd v City Link Transport Holdings Ltd [1999] EWCA Civ 1822

In a dispute over an earlier agreement the parties negotiated a settlement under which the defendant offered to pay £13,500 plus a refund of carriage charges of £7.50 plus VAT. The claimant then accepted by letter. The defendant argued that the acceptance was invalid because the claimant's letter stated that VAT should be paid on the whole amount and therefore was a counter offer.

The court held that the whole correspondence between the parties should be considered in deciding if there was a contract. It held that the claimant had clearly accepted the defendant's offer in its letter and a binding contract resulted from the defendant's offer. The defendant could not escape its own clearly accepted obligations just because the claimant restated them in a contrary way.

This shows that courts will not allow parties to introduce relatively meaningless counter offers that are unlikely to be challenged in order to get the best of both worlds and be able to rely on either the original offer or the counter offer as suits them best.

Brogden v Metropolitan Railway Co (1877) 2 App Cas 666

The parties had a long-standing informal arrangement for supply of coal. They then decided to make it formal and a draft contract was sent to Brogden by the Railway Company.

Brogden inserted the name of an arbitrator into a section left blank for that purpose, signed it and returned it. The Railway Company secretary signed it without looking at it. Brogden continued to supply coal and was paid for deliveries. After some conflict over other matters Brogden tried to avoid his obligations, arguing that there was no contract because of a counter offer by the Railway Company, which then sued.

The court accepted that technically the insertion of the arbitrator's name was a counter offer, but held that this had no real effect as coal was still supplied and paid for. The parties had accepted the counter offer as part of the agreement and the contract was valid.

1.2.2 The 'battle of the forms'

British Steel Corporation v Cleveland Bridge and Engineering Co. **[1984] 1 All ER 504**

Cleveland Bridge was sub-contracted to build the steel framework for a bank in Saudi Arabia. This required four steel nodes which it asked BSC to make. BSC wanted a disclaimer of liability for loss caused by late delivery but Cleveland Bridge would not accept this and so no written agreement was made. BSC still delivered three nodes, but the fourth was delayed owing to a strike. Cleveland Bridge refused to pay and argued breach of contract for late delivery of the fourth. BSC sued successfully on a *quantum meruit*.

Because of the total disagreement over a major term, the judge found it impossible to recognise that there was a meaningful agreement but still enforced payment for the three nodes.

The rules on offer and acceptance can cause such problems, particularly if standard forms conflict. In *New Zealand Shipping Co. Ltd v A.M. Satterthwaite & Co. Ltd (The Eurymedon)* [1975] AC 154 Lord Wilberforce said 'It is only the precise analysis of this complex of relations into the classical offer and acceptance with identifiable consideration that seems to present difficulty [but] English law, having committed itself to a rather technical and schematic doctrine of contract, in application takes a practical approach, often at the cost of forcing the facts to fit uneasily into the marked slots of offer and acceptance'. Lord Denning in *Butler Machine Tool Co Ltd v Ex-Cell-O Corporation* [1979] 1 WLR 401 stated that where standard forms differ significantly then 'The terms and conditions of both parties are to be construed together. If they can be reconciled … to give harmonious result, all well and good. If the differences are irreconcilable, so that they are mutually contradictory, then the conflicting terms may have to be scrapped and replaced by a reasonable implication'. This is a radical solution not accepted by most judges although they recognise the need to reconcile the basic rules of contract law and the demands of modern business.

1.2.3 Communication of the acceptance

CP ***Felthouse v Bindley* [1863] 142 ER 1037**

An uncle and nephew negotiated the sale of the nephew's horse. The uncle said 'If I hear no more from you I shall consider the horse mine at £30: 15s'. The nephew's stock was then auctioned. The auctioneer failed to withdraw the horse from the sale as the nephew had instructed and it was sold to another party. To claim conversion in tort against the auctioneer the uncle had to prove that a contract existed for the sale and purchase of the horse. His action failed.

The nephew had not actually accepted the offer to buy and the court would not accept silence as any indication of acceptance.

KB ***Adams v Lindsell*** **[1818] 106 ER 250**

Wool was offered for sale and, because the parties were not in close contact, the seller demanded acceptance by post. The prospective purchaser responded by letter on the same day that he received the offer. However, his letter of acceptance was not received until long afterwards by which time the seller had sold the wool. The purchaser sued successfully for breach of contract.

The court considered the problems of contracting at a distance at the time and the possible injustices caused by delays in the postal system. It held that where the post is the normal anticipated means of acceptance, acceptance occurs at the time of posting and a binding contract is formed then, not when the letter is received.

It has been stated that the letter of acceptance would also need to be properly stamped and addressed for the rule to apply.

Household Fire Insurance v Grant (1879) 4 ExD 216

Grant made a postal application to buy shares. The company then sent him a letter of allotment by post, the established method of signifying acceptance. This letter was posted but never received by Grant. The insurance company later went into liquidation. As a shareholder Grant was liable to creditors of the company for the face value of his shares. Grant's argued that he was not a shareholder and should not be liable but failed.

The court held that Grant become a shareholder even though he was unaware of it because he never received the letter of allotment. The contract was formed at the moment of posting and it was irrelevant to Grant's liability that he had never received the letter. His name and shareholding was registered in the company's name and his liability as a shareholder was evident from this.

Entores Ltd v Miles Far East Corporation [1955] 2 QB 327

Dutch agents of an American company accepted by telex an offer for sale and purchase of equipment made by a British company. In a later dispute the claimant needed to prove that the contract was made in England in order to sue successfully.

The court held that, because of the method of communicating, the contract was actually made in England when the telex was received not when it was transmitted in Holland.

Lord Denning explained why the postal rule could not apply '[if] I shout an offer to a man across a river ... but I do not hear his reply because it is drowned by an aircraft flying overhead there is no contract at that moment. If he wishes to make a contract he must wait till the aircraft is gone and then shout back his acceptance so that I can hear what he says. Not till I have the answer am I bound'.

***Brinkibon v Stahag Stahl* [1983] AC 34**

The alleged acceptance by telex was received out of office hours. The question was whether this was valid to form a contract.

The court held that acceptance had to be communicated, so could only be effective to create the contract once the office reopened.

Lord Wilberforce said 'No universal rule can cover all such cases; they must be resolved by reference to the intention of the parties, ... sound business practice and ... by a judgment where the risk should lie'.

Faxes, e-mail, and use of the Internet are even more modern forms of communication and are covered by the Consumer Protection (Distance Selling) Regulations 2000 and the E-Commerce (EU Directive) Regulations 2003.

1.3 Consideration

1.3.1 Defining 'consideration'

HL ***Dunlop Pneumatic Tyre Co. v Selfridge & Co.***
[1915] AC 847

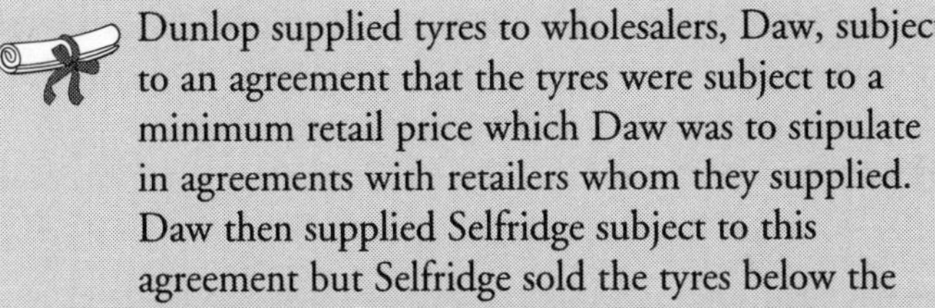

Dunlop supplied tyres to wholesalers, Daw, subject to an agreement that the tyres were subject to a minimum retail price which Daw was to stipulate in agreements with retailers whom they supplied. Daw then supplied Selfridge subject to this agreement but Selfridge sold the tyres below the minimum retail price. Dunlop sued Selfridge to enforce the agreement but failed.

The action could not succeed because there was no privity between Dunlop and Selfridge and neither had given any consideration to the other to make the agreement imposed by Dunlop enforceable against a third party to their agreement with Daw.

The House of Lords approved Sir Frederick Pollock's definition of 'consideration' from *Principles of Contract*: 'an act of forbearance or the promise thereof is the price for which the promise of the other is bought, and the promise thus given for value is enforceable'.

This is the modern definition of 'consideration' based on exchange. It contrasts with the previous accepted definition in *Currie v Misa* (1875) 1 App Cas 554 of 'some right, interest, profit or benefit accruing to one party, or some forbearance, detriment, loss or responsibility given, suffered or undertaken by the other'.

1.3.2 Sufficiency and adequacy of consideration

QBD ***Thomas v Thomas*** **[1842] 2 QB 851**

Before he died Thomas expressed a wish that his wife should be allowed to remain in his house although there was no mention of this in his will. The executors carried out this wish but charged the widow a nominal ground rent of £1 per year. When they later tried to dispossess her they failed.

The payment of ground rent, however small and inadequate, was sufficient consideration to bind the executors to the moral obligation that they had accepted.

Patteson J based his reasoning on benefit/detriment theory: 'Consideration means something which is of value in the eye of the law, moving from the plaintiff: it may be some benefit to the plaintiff or some detriment to the defendant'.

HL ***Chappell v Nestlé*** **[1960] AC 87**

Nestlé had offered a record, normally retailing at 6/8d (not quite equivalent to 34p now), for 1/6d (7.5p now) plus three chocolate bar wrappers, to promote their chocolate, although on receipt the wrappers were thrown away. Holders of the copyright of the record sued in order to obtain royalties from each record given away. To succeed they needed to show that the gift was part of a contract with customers and to show this they had to prove that the wrappers amounted to consideration.

The House of Lords accepted that the wrappers were good consideration because the promotion was designed to sell more chocolate bars so there was a tangible commercial value to Nestlé.

Lord Somervell said 'It is said … the wrappers are of no value to … Nestlé … This I would have thought to be irrelevant. A … party can stipulate for what consideration he chooses. A peppercorn does not cease to be good consideration if it is established that the promisee does not like pepper and will throw away the corn'.

White v Bluett **(1853) 23 LJ Ex 36**

A father held IOUs for his son's debts. The father died and his executors tried to recover the money from the son who argued unsuccessfully that he was not bound to pay because of an agreement with his father that the debts would be forgotten if the son promised not to complain about being left out of his father's will.

The son's promise was held to be too intangible and too unreal to provide consideration for the father's promise to forgo the debts.

Ward v Byham **[1956] 1 WLR 496**

A father of an illegitimate child had promised its mother money towards its upkeep if she would keep the child 'well looked after and happy'. The woman sued when the father failed to pay. His argument, that the mother would be doing nothing more than she was already bound by law to do in looking after the child, failed.

The court was prepared to enforce the agreement. Since there is no obligation in law to keep a child happy, this was more than the mother was bound to do, had real value and was consideration.

Stilk v Myrick [1809] 170 ER 1168 (p22).

1.3.3 Past consideration

***Re McArdle* [1951] Ch 669**

A son and his wife lived in his mother's house. On the woman's death the house would be inherited by the son and her three other children. The son's wife paid for substantial repairs and improvements to the property. The mother then made her four children sign an agreement to reimburse the daughter-in-law out of her estate. When the woman died and the children refused to keep this promise the daughter-in-law sued to enforce the agreement.

The wife failed as her 'consideration' for the promise to reimburse her was past. It was not done as a result of the agreement to repay her but came before it. Past consideration is no consideration.

Roscorla v Thomas [1842] 3 QB 234.

***Re Casey's Patent* [1892] 1 Ch 104**

Joint owners of a patent wrote to the claimant, agreeing to give him a third share of the patents for work done in managing the patents. The claimant then wished to enforce this agreement but the owners then argued that the agreement was actually in respect of his past services and so was unenforceable for past consideration. He had in fact supplied no consideration following the agreement.

Bowen LJ held that there was both an implied promise and a legitimate commercial expectation that in managing the patents the claimant should be paid for the work done. The later agreement to pay was therefore enforceable.

Lampleigh v Braithwaite [1615] 80 ER 255.

1.3.4 Consideration passing from both sides

***Tweddle v Atkinson* [1861] 121 ER 762**

The fathers of a young couple who intended to marry agreed in writing with each other that they would each settle a sum of money on the couple. The woman's father died before giving the money and the young man then sued the woman's father's executors when they refused to hand over the money.

Despite being named in the agreement, the young man was unsuccessful. He was not an actual party to the agreement and had given no consideration for the agreement himself.

This is clearly an unfair consequence of the privity rule and the rule that consideration must move from the promisee.

Contracts (Rights of Third Parties) Act 1999. This case would now be dealt with differently under the Act.

1.3.5 Performance of existing duties

***Stilk v Myrick* [1809] 170 ER 1168**

Two members of a ship's crew of 11 deserted. The captain promised the rest that they could share the men's wages if they sailed the ship safely back to port. The ship's owner then refused to make the extra payments and the sailors sued unsuccessfully.

The sailors were held to be bound by their contract to cope with the normal contingencies of the voyage which could include desertions, and therefore had given no extra consideration for the captain's promise to pay them extra wages.

Lord Ellenborough explained 'There was no consideration for the ulterior pay promised to the mariners who remained with the ship. … they had undertaken to do all that they could under all emergencies of the voyage … the desertion of a part of the crew is … an emergency … as much as their death; and those who remain are bound by the terms of their original contract to exert themselves to the utmost to bring the ship safely to her destined port'.

Hartley v Ponsonby (1857) 7 E & B 872 – here there was consideration because the claimant was doing more than he was already contractually bound to do.

HL ***Glassbrook Bros v Glamorgan County Council*** **[1925] AC 270**

When miners were on strike and picketing the colliery the pit owner asked the local police for extra protection and agreed to a payment in return. He then refused to pay when the strike was over and argued that the police were doing nothing more than their public duty to protect his pit and was sued successfully.

The court held that, because of the request, the police had provided more men than they would normally have done which was consideration for the promise of payment.

PC ***Pao On v Lau Yiu Long*** **[1980] AC 614**

Pao and Lau owned companies. The major asset of Pao's company was a building that Lau wished to purchase. Lau's company contracted to buy Pao's in return for a large number of shares in Lau's company. To avoid the potential damage from such large trading in shares, Lau inserted a clause in the contract that Pao should retain 60% of the shares for at least one year, (Agreement 1) Pao wanted a guarantee that the shares would not fall in value and another agreement was made at the same time by which Lau would buy back 60% of the shares at $2.50 each. Pao later realised that this might benefit Lau more if the shares rose in value and so refused to carry out the contract unless the subsidiary arrangement was scrapped and replaced with a straightforward indemnity by Lau against a fall in the value of the shares. Lau could have sued at this point for breach of contract but, fearing a resulting loss of public confidence in his company, agreed to the new terms (Agreement 2). When the value of the shares did fall Lau refused to honour the agreement and Pao tried to enforce the indemnity. Lao offered two defences. Firstly, the indemnity agreement (Agreement 2) was past consideration. Secondly, Pao had given no consideration for that agreement as he was only doing what he was bound to do under the first agreement, pass the company in return for the shares.

In response to Lau's first defence the Privy Council applied the rule in *Lampleigh v Braithwaite.* Lau's demand that Pao should not sell 60% of the shares for one year was a request for a service that carried an implied promise to pay. This promise was later supported by the actual promise to indemnify Pao. Lau's second defence also failed. Pao gave consideration by continuing with the contract, which protected the credibility and financial standing of Lau's company and the price payable in return was the indemnity.

CA ***Williams v Roffey Bros & Nicholls Contractors Ltd***
[1990] 1 All ER 512

Roffey Bros builders sub-contracted the carpentry on a number of flats they were building to Williams for £20,000. Williams had under-quoted for the work and ran into financial difficulties. Because there was a delay clause in Roffey's building contract, meaning they would have to pay money to the client if the flats were not built on time, they promised to pay Williams another £10,300 if he would complete the carpentry on time. When Williams completed the work and Roffey failed to pay extra, his claim to the money succeeded.

Even though Williams only did what he was already contractually bound to do, Roffey were gaining the extra commercial benefit of not having to pay under the delay clause. Williams was providing consideration for their promise to pay him more for the work merely by completing his existing obligations on time.

Purchas LJ distinguished the case from *Stilk v Myrick*: 'I consider that the modern approach to the question of consideration would be that where there were benefits derived by each party to a contract of variation even though one party did not suffer a detriment this would not be fatal to establishing sufficient consideration to support the agreement. If both parties benefit from an agreement it is not necessary that each also suffers a detriment.'

The case was distinguished from *Stilk v Myrick* but there seems to be very little difference. Williams was only doing what he was contractually bound to do and the extra benefit, even though it may have commercial value, appears neither real nor tangible.

1.3.6 Pinnel's Rule and promissory estoppel

CA ***D and C Builders v Rees*** **[1965] 3 All ER 837**

Builders were owed £482 for work that they had completed for the Reeses. They waited several months for payment and when they were in danger of going out of business, they reluctantly accepted an offer by the Reeses to pay £300 in full satisfaction of the debt. They then sued for the balance and succeeded.

Because of Pinnel's rule (an agreement to accept part payment of a debt never satisfies the whole debt), they were not bound by the agreement to accept less. Lord Denning identified that in any case this was extracted from them under pressure.

Foakes v Beer (1884) 9 App Cas 605; and see also **5.3.2**.

KB ***Central London Property Trust Ltd v High Trees House Ltd*** **[1947] KB 130**

From 1937 the defendant leased a block of flats in Wimbledon from the claimant to sub-let to tenants. During the war it was impossible to find tenants so the defendant was unable to pay the rent. The claimant agreed to accept half rent, which the defendants then paid. By 1945 the flats were all let and the claimant wanted the rent returned to its former level and sued for the last two quarters.

The decision is pure application of Pinnel's Rule: an agreement to accept part payment of a debt never satisfies the debt as a whole.

Lord Denning said *in obiter* that if they had tried to sue for the extra rent for the whole period of the war promissory estoppel would have prevented them from going back on the promise on which the defendants had relied. He stated: 'In such cases … the promise must be honoured … the logical consequence … is that a promise to accept a smaller sum in discharge of a larger debt if acted upon, is binding notwithstanding the absence of consideration.'

As this suggested that there was no need to prove consideration in *Combe v Combe* [1951] 2 KB 215 Lord Denning had to explain estoppel in more detail: 'Where one party has by his words or conduct made … a promise or assurance which was intended to affect the legal conditions between them and be acted on accordingly, then once the other party has … acted on it the one who gave the promise cannot afterwards be allowed to revert to the previous legal relations as if no such promise had been made.'

***Re Selectmove* [1995] 2 All ER 531**

A company that owed tax to the Inland Revenue offered to pay the debt in instalments. It was told that it would be contacted by the IRC if this was unsatisfactory and began to pay off its debt by instalments. The IRC then insisted on all arrears of tax being paid immediately or it would begin winding-up procedures against the company. The company unsuccessfully argued on the basis of *Williams v Roffey* that its promise to carry out an existing obligation was good consideration for the agreement to pay by instalments because the IRC got the benefit of all the money being paid.

The court distinguished *Williams v Roffey* since that case involved provision of goods and services not payment of an existing debt so the precedent in *Foakes v Beer* was applied and the IRC was not bound by the agreement to accept payment by instalments.

This seems inconsistent with the reasoning in *Williams v Roffey*.

1.4 Intention to create legal relations

1.4.1 Social and domestic arrangements

***Balfour v Balfour* [1919] 2 KB 571**

A man was on overseas service, but his wife was ill and had to remain in England so he promised her £30 per month allowance but did not pay. Later he suggested separation, his wife petitioned for divorce and her claim to payment of the allowance failed.

The court held that the agreement was made while the couple were still amicable and not in contemplation of divorce. It was thus a purely domestic arrangement, beyond the competence of the court to interfere with and not legally enforceable.

Atkin LJ explained: 'arrangements … made between husband and wife … are not contracts because the parties did not intend that they should be attended by legal consequences. The small courts of this country would have to be multiplied one hundredfold if [they] did result in … legal obligations'.

CA ***Merritt v Merritt*** **[1970] 1 WLR 1211**

A man had deserted his wife for another woman. The home was in joint names and the man promised his wife an income of £40 per month if she continued to pay the outstanding mortgage. She sued successfully when she kept her promise but the husband failed to.

The court held that there was an intention to be legally bound by the agreement. This was supported by the fact that when the arrangement was made the wife had got her husband to put in writing that he would transfer title in the property to her on completion of the mortgage, which he had not in fact done. The wife's action for recognition of sole title rights was successful.

Lord Denning identified the difference from *Balfour v Balfour*: 'It is altogether different when the parties are not living in amity but are separated or about to separate. They then bargain keenly. They do not rely on honourable understandings. They want everything cut and dried ... they intend to create legal relations.'

***Simpkins v Pays* [1955] 1 WLR 975**

A lodger and two members of the household where he lodged entered newspaper competitions in the lodger's name but all paid equal shares of the entry money. There was a clear understanding that they would share any winnings and so, when they won £750 and the lodger refused to share the winnings, the other two sued.

The court rejected the lodger's argument that the arrangement was domestic and did not give rise to a legal relationship. The presence of a detriment, the payment for entering the competitions meant that the parties had intended that the arrangement was legally binding.

***Parker v Clarke* [1960] 1 WLR 286**

A young couple were persuaded by an older couple to sell their house in order to move in with the older couple, with the promise also that they would inherit property on the death of the old couple. When the two couples eventually fell out and the young couple was asked to leave, their action for damages succeeded.

The judge held that giving up their security was an indication that the arrangement was intended to be legally binding and the presumption usually applied to domestic agreements was rebutted.

***Jones v Padavatton* [1969] 1 WLR 328**

A woman persuaded her daughter to give up a highly paid job in New York to study for the Bar in England and then return to practise in Trinidad where the mother lived. In return she agreed to pay her daughter an allowance. The daughter found it difficult to manage on the allowance and the woman then bought a house for the daughter to live in, part of which the daughter could let to supplement her income. They quarrelled so the mother sought repossession. The daughter's defence that there was a contract failed.

The court could find no intent and held that the second agreement was too vague to be considered contractually binding.

1.4.2 Commercial and business dealings

QBD ***Edwards v Skyways Ltd* [1969] 1 WLR 349**

An employer failed to pay an agreed *ex gratia* payment during a redundancy situation and the claimant sued successfully.

The court held that, while *ex gratia* payments are generally without any obligation, the agreement was binding because of the context in which it was made which indicated legal enforceability.

HL

***Esso Petroleum Co. Ltd v Commissioners of Customs and Excise* [1976] 1 All ER 117**

During a World Cup, Esso gave free World Cup coins with every four gallons of petrol. The Customs and Excise department wanted to claim purchase tax from the transaction and needed to show that the arrangement was contractual, the purchase of petrol being the consideration for the free coin, and also therefore that there was an intention to create a legal relationship.

The House of Lords was divided. The dissenting judges held that the transaction was too trivial to be contractual but the majority held that, since Esso aimed to gain more business from the promotion, there was an intention to be bound by the arrangement.

Lord Simon said: 'Esso [designed the scheme] for their commercial advantage … to attract the custom of motorists. The whole transaction took place in a setting of business relations. [and] it seems … undesirable to allow a commercial promoter to claim that what he has done is … not intended to create legal relations. The … evidence suggests that Esso contemplated that … there would be a large commercial advantage to themselves from the scheme.'

Rose and Frank Co v J R Crompton & Bros [1923] 2 KB 261; [1925] AC 445

A firm sold paper for tissue manufacturers, as their New York agents. In the contract the firm gained sales and distribution rights for three years, with an option to extend the time. A clause in the contract stated that, in the event of dispute, there would be no reference to the courts but the parties would be bound by an 'honourable pledge'. This in effect stated that the agreement was not a formal agreement but a genuine statement of the purpose of the agreement between them and of the intention of the parties to pursue that purpose with mutual cooperation. The contract was extended, but the manufacturers then terminated it too early and refused to process orders made before the termination. The claimant sued on the basis of the broken agency agreement and also for the failure to deliver the goods already ordered.

The Court of Appeal, ignoring the agency agreement, held the termination lawful because of the 'honour pledge' clause. The House of Lords accepted that it could apply to the agreement as a whole, which could be terminated without legal consequences. It would not accept that the clause could apply also to the specific transactions and reversed the Court of Appeal on those. This was because a separate contract could be inferred from the conduct of the parties, enforceable without reference to the original agreement.

Kleinwort Benson Ltd v Malaysian Mining Corporation
[1989] 1 WLR 379

Kleinwort lent £10 million to Metals Ltd, which was a subsidiary company of the Malaysian Mining Corporation. The parent company (MMC) would not guarantee this loan but instead issued a comfort letter stating that their intention was to ensure that at all times Metals Ltd had sufficient funds available for repayment of the loan. When Metals Ltd went out of business without repaying Kleinwort the latter then sued the parent company. Its action was based on the existence of the comfort letter but failed.

The court held that if Kleinwort had actually required a guarantee of repayment then they should have insisted on one before engaging in the transaction rather than accepting a mere comfort letter.

CHAPTER 2

CAPACITY

Capacity

Corporations are limited in their capacity to contract by their objects clause *Rolled Steel Products (Holdings) Ltd v British Steel Corporation*

Minors are bound to pay a reasonable price for necessaries actually delivered *Nash v Inman*

And employment contracts substantially for their benefit *De Francesco v Barnum*

But can avoid contracts of continuous obligation *Steinberg v Scala (Leeds) Ltd*

In contracts unenforceable against a minor restitution can be used to prevent a minor's unjust enrichment *Leslie (R) Ltd v Sheill*

2.1 Corporations and capacity

HL

Ashbury Railway Carriage Co Ltd v Riche
(1875) LR 7 HL 653

An engineering company was formed to build railway stock. The directors contracted to assign a concession that they had bought to build a railway in Belgium to a Belgian company. It failed to honour the agreement and the Belgian company sought to enforce it.

Ashbury's objects clause did not allow it to build railways so the contract was *ultra vires* (beyond its powers) and therefore void.

Rolled Steel Products (Holdings) Ltd v British Steel Corporation [1985] 2 WLR 908

The owners of Rolled Steel also owned Scottish Sheet Steel which it owed £400,000 in debentures. Scottish Sheet Steel was a steel stockholder and bought from BSC which it owed £800,000. Rolled Steel owned land which BSC asked for a charge on to guarantee Scottish Sheet Steel's debt. Rolled Steel did so but failed to pay the debts. In liquidation the land was sold for £1.2 million but paid out on costs etc. The liquidator challenged the validity of the debenture and the guarantee since Rolled Steel, while it had ancillary power to give security for debts and to give guarantees did it here on behalf of another company and thus for an unlawful purpose.

Nevertheless the House of Lords held that the transaction was lawful as the ancillary power was within the company's capacity.

In the Court of Appeal **Slade LJ** explained 'if the transaction [relies on] a power which is capable of being exercised for purposes within the objects, then it will not become *ultra vires* merely because the transaction is entered into for purposes outside the objects'.

The case seems to contradict previous law. The purpose of the *ultra vires* doctrine was to protect parties from the effects of unlawful dealing but companies could use it to defeat claims by legitimate creditors. It also limited the ability of companies to expand their operations so objects clauses were often very widely drafted. New EU-led provisions in s 35 of the Companies Act 1985 remedy this.

2.2 Capacity and minors' contracts

Chapple v Cooper **(1844) 3 M & W 252**

A minor's husband died and she contracted with undertakers for his funeral but later refused to pay for it, claiming that she had no capacity to contract. The undertakers sued for the cost.

She was liable to pay. The funeral was substantially for her benefit and was necessary as she had an obligation to bury her husband.

CA ***Nash v Inman*** **[1908] 2 KB 1**

A Cambridge undergraduate, the son of an architect, was supplied with clothes worth £122 by a Saville Row tailor; including 11 'fancy waistcoats' costing 2 guineas each (£2.10p). The tailor sued when the student's father refused to pay for the clothing.

On appeal the court accepted that the supply of such clothing could be appropriate to the undergraduate's station but was not a necessary as the minor already had an adequate supply of clothes.

The test seems outdated but is still relevant in certain contracts.

By s 3 of the Sale of Goods Act 1979 'Where necessaries are sold and delivered to a minor … he must pay a reasonable price'.

***Clements v London and North Western Railway Company* [1894] 2 QB 482**

The claimant minor gained employment as a railway porter for the defendant and agreed to join the company's insurance scheme as a result of which he relinquished rights under the Employer's Liability Act 1880. When the minor was injured at work the statutory scheme would have been of more benefit since it allowed compensation for a wider range of accidents. The minor argued that he was not bound by his employer's scheme but failed.

The court held that, viewing the contract as a whole, it was substantially to his benefit and enforceable.

***De Francesco v Barnum* (1890) 45 Ch D 430**

A 14-year-old entered a seven-year dancing apprenticeship with De Francesco. In the apprenticeship deed she agreed to be at his total disposal, to accept no professional work without his express approval and not to marry without his permission.

He had no obligation to maintain her or to employ her, but if he did the pay was very low, and he could terminate the arrangement without notice. She accepted other work. De Francesco sought to prevent it and failed.

The apprenticeship deed was held to be unfair and unenforceable against her. It was not substantially for her benefit.

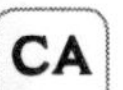

***Steinberg v Scala (Leeds) Ltd* [1923] 2 Ch 452**

A minor was allotted company shares for which she had made the first payment. She was unable to meet the further payments and sought to repudiate the contract and to recover the money that she had already paid. She succeeded on the first but not the second.

The court accepted that the contract was voidable so that her name could be removed from the register of shareholders and she would have no further liability for the company. However, it would not grant return of her money. There was no failure of consideration. While she had received no dividends or attended any meetings of shareholders, she had been registered as a shareholder and received everything she was entitled to under the contract.

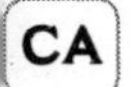

***Leslie (R) Ltd v Sheill* [1914] 3 KB 607**

A minor fraudulently misrepresented his age to get a loan from the claimant who then sought repayment of the loan.

The court held that at common law the claimant could not recover the amount of the loan since this would have the effect of enforcing a void contract. It also identified that had the contract involved goods, the minor would have been obliged in equity to return them, but that restitution could not apply in the same way to the money.

Sumner LJ explained: 'when an infant obtained an advantage by falsely stating himself to be of full age, equity required him to restore his ill-gotten gains, or to release the party deceived from obligations or acts in law induced by the fraud, but scrupulously stopped short of enforcing against him a contractual obligation, entered into while he was an infant, even by means of fraud.'

The role of equity is now replaced by s 3 of the Minors' Contracts Act 1987 which provides that it is no longer vital to prove fraud against a minor to recover property from him provided the court can identify an unjust enrichment and it is equitable to do so.

CHAPTER 3

THIRD PARTY RIGHTS AND PRIVITY OF CONTRACT

Third party rights and privity

Nobody can sue or be sued on a contract which they have given no consideration for *Dunlop Pneumatic Tyre Co Ltd v Selfridge & Co Ltd*
The doctrine will not apply where a trust is created *Affreteurs Reunis S.A. v Walford (Walford's Case)*
Or where a collateral promise can be relied on *Shanklin Pier v Detel Products Ltd*
But statute cannot be used out of context to avoid the privity rule *Beswick v Beswick*

3.1.The basic rule and its effects

CA ***Price v Easton*** **[1833] 110 ER 518**

The defendant had agreed with another party that if that party did specified work he would pay £19 to the claimant, a third party to the contract. The work was completed but the defendant failed to pay. The claimant sued unsuccessfully to enforce the provision.

The court held that since the claimant gave no consideration for the agreement and was not a party to it he had no enforceable rights.

HL ***Dunlop Pneumatic Tyre Co. Ltd v Selfridge & Co. Ltd*** **[1915] AC 847**

Dew & Co., wholesalers, contracted to buy tyres from Dunlop, tyre manufacturers, with an express undertaking in the contract that it would not sell the tyres below prices fixed by Dunlop. Dew & Co. also agreed to contract on the same price fixing agreements with clients that they sold on to. Dew sold tyres to Selfridge on those terms but Selfridge broke the agreement and sold tyres at discount prices. Dunlop sought an injunction against Selfridge but failed.

The court rejected the claim because of lack of privity. (The case would now be subject to the Restrictive Trade Practices Act.)

Lord Haldane said: 'only a person who is a party to a contract can sue on it. Our law knows nothing of a *jus quaesitum tertio* arising by way of contract. Such a right may be conferred … under a trust, but [not] on a stranger to a contract as a right to enforce the contract *in personam…*'. **Lord Dunedin** said: 'the effect … in the present case is to make it possible for a person to snap his fingers at a bargain deliberately made, a bargain not unfair in itself, and which the person seeking to enforce it has a legitimate interest to enforce'.

3.2 Exceptions to the strict rule

HL ***Affreteurs Reunis S.A. v Walford (Walford's Case)*** **[1919] AC 801**

Walford, a broker, negotiated an agreement between a charter party and the owner of the vessel to be chartered. He was obviously not a party to the agreement between the owners of the vessel and the charter party. The contract included a clause that Walford was to receive 3% commission from the ship owner for securing the agreement. The owner failed to pay and Walford sued successfully.

The court held that a trust was created because Walford was named as receiving a benefit under the agreement.

The courts will not accept that a trust is created unless there is a clear intention to create one. So it must be satisfied that the interest claimed conforms to the general character of a trust: see *Green v Russell* [1959] 2 QB 226.

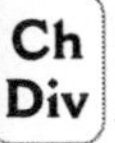

Tulk v Moxhay [1848] 41 ER 1143

Tulk owned land in London which he sold, subject to an express undertaking that it could not be used to build property on. The land was re-sold many times, each time subject to the same undertaking, until Moxhay bought it. Moxhay knew of the limitation but still intended to build on it. Tulk successfully sought an injunction.

The court accepted that it would be inequitable for Moxhay to buy, knowing of the restriction but intending to ignore it. It granted the injunction despite Moxhay never having been a party to it.

Taddy v Sterious [1904] 1 Ch 354 where the device could not be used to enforce an agreement controlling the pricing of goods.

Alfred McAlpine Construction Ltd v Panatown Ltd
(1998) 88 BLR 67

McAlpine contracted with Panatown to design and build a multi-storey car park. McAlpine also entered into a 'duty of care deed' with Unex Investment Properties Ltd (UIPL), the actual owners of the site. Panatown sued McAlpine, claiming that the building was so defective that it would need to be rebuilt. McAlpine countered that Panatown was not the owner of the site and, as only UIPL had suffered loss, Panatown could claim only nominal damages and UIPL nothing since it was not a party to the contract.

The Court of Appeal applied the rule in *Dunlop v Lambert* (that a contracting party can recover damages even though a third party suffers the actual loss). It accepted that the deed with UIPL indicated that contractual rights were given to the third party but that on the facts, since all accounts had to be settled between Panatown and McAlpine, Panatown must have the right to sue on behalf of the third party. A split House of Lords held that the 'duty of care deed' with UIPL prevented Panatown from suing. The deed meant that the third party was given a specific remedy by the contract even though this remedy was more limited than that which would have been available under Panatown's breach of contract action. The majority accepted the narrow principle from *Dunlop v Lambert* as a recognised exception but felt its application was inappropriate and unnecessary in the case because of the 'duty of care deed'.

QBD **_Snelling v John G Snelling Ltd_ [1973] 1 QB 87**

Three brothers were directors of a private company. The brothers also financed the company through loans. The company borrowed money from a finance company and the brothers agreed that, until the finance company loan was repaid, if any of them resigned their directorship in the company, they would forfeit the amount of their loan to the company which was not party to this agreement. One brother then left the company, resigned his directorship and sued the company for return of his loan. The other two brothers applied to join the company as defendants and counterclaimed on the basis that the forfeiture agreement should apply.

The court agreed to this. Even though the company was not a party to the agreement the brothers and the company were in effect the same so that all parties to the action were present in court.

PC **_New Zealand Shipping Co. Ltd v A.M. Satterthwaite & Co. Ltd (The Eurymedon)_ [1975] AC 154**

Carriers contracted with the consignors of goods to ship drilling equipment. The contract included a limitation clause which also extended to any servant or agent of the carriers. The carriers hired stevedores to unload the equipment, and through the stevedores' negligence substantial damage was caused to the equipment. The stevedores successfully argued that this clause limited their liability.

The court identified that there was a contractual relationship based on agency and that the stevedores could rely on the clause.

Apart from the stevedores having only a tenuous link to the contract it is also hard to see any consideration that they had provided.

KB ***Shanklin Pier v Detel Products Ltd*** **[1951] 2 KB 854**

The claimant owned a pier and was assured by the defendant paint manufacturer that its paint was durable, weather resistant and suitable to paint the pier, that it would not flake or peel and would last at least seven years. The pier owner, relying on the promises, hired painting contractors to paint the pier, instructing them to use Detel's paint. The paint was unsuitable and peeled within three months. The pier owner could not sue the painters who completed the work professionally. The quality of the paint was the sole fault of the defects. The pier owner was not a party to the contract between the painters and Detel for the purchase of the paint but sued successfully on the collateral warranties made by Detel.

The court held Detel liable on the promise despite apparent lack of privity in the painting contract. It had made a collateral promise on which the pier owners were entitled to rely and thus could sue.

Technically it can be argued that the collateral contract is not an exception to the privity rule. The court in fact is identifying a contract between the two parties based on the collateral promise even though the relationship seems indirect. The party making the promise gains the benefit of selling its goods because its promise has induced the other party to enter into a separate contract with another party and it is bound by this promise.

HL **_Beswick v Beswick_ [1968] AC 58**

A coal merchant sold his business to his nephew. The contract contained two specific undertakings from the nephew, to provide his uncle with an income till the uncle died, and that after the uncle's death he should provide the man's widow with a weekly annuity. The uncle died intestate and the nephew made only one payment to his aunt. She sued as administratrix of her dead husband's estate and on her own behalf in trying to enforce the agreement for the weekly annuity. While the agreement was a condition in the sale of the business to the nephew, the widow clearly lacked privity to the agreement, having provided no consideration for it. In pursuing her own action she attempted to use a provision in s 56(1) of the Law of Property Act 1925 stating that 'A person may take an immediate interest or other interest in land other property … although he may not be named as a party to the conveyance or other instrument'.

The Court of Appeal allowed both claims. In the widow's own claim under s 56, Lord Denning MR held that since the 1925

Act at s 205 provided that 'unless the context otherwise requires … Property includes … real or personal property' s 56 exempted the widow from the privity rule, thus creating another major exception. The House of Lords upheld specific performance of the husband's contract with John, but rejected the Court of Appeal's reasoning in the wife's claim under s 56. It held that as the Act referred only to real property (land) it could not be applied to purely personal property.

Lord Hodson said: 's 56 … does not have the revolutionary effect claimed for it … that the context does require a limited meaning to be given to the word "property" in the section'.

CHAPTER 4

THE CONTENTS OF A CONTRACT

Terms:
Must distinguish between terms and 'mere representations' *Bissett v Wilkinson*
Terms must be incorporated into the contract *Oscar Chess Ltd v Williams*
Parties are bound by contracts they have signed *L'Estrange v Graucob*
Terms can be implied into a contract e.g. for business efficacy *The Moorcock*
But this must represent the presumed intention of both parties *Shell (UK) Ltd v Lostock Garages Ltd*
Terms can also be implied by common law *Liverpool City Council v Irwin*
As well as by statute e.g. Sale of Goods Act 1979 *Grant v Australian Knitting Mills*
Terms can be 'conditions' going to the root of the contract and allowing for repudiation as well as an action for damages *Poussard v Spiers and Pond*
Or warranties only giving rise to damages *Bettini v Gye*
The description given to terms must comply with their effect in breach *Schuler (L) AG v Wickman Machine Tool Sales Ltd*
With innominate terms the remedy depends on the effect of the breach *Reardon Smith Line v Hansen-Tangen*

Contents

Exclusion clauses:
Exclusion clauses may affect consumers adversely so, to be incorporated, the party subject to them must be aware of them *Olley v Marlborough Court Hotels*
Prior dealings are only relevant if consistent *McCutcheon v MacBrayne*
They are not incorporated if in a form not easily recognisable as contractual *Curtis v Chemical Cleaning Co*
And the party seeking to rely on them may have to make every effort to communicate to the party subject to them *Thornton v Shoe Lane Parking*
The *contra preferentem* rule means any ambiguity works against the party inserting the clause *Hollier v Rambler Motors*
Where parties of equal bargaining strength negotiate freely and the clause is clear and unambiguous the clause stands *Ailsa Craig Fishing v Malvern Fishing*
Under the Unfair Contract Terms Act 1977 insertion of a clause may have to satisfy a test of reasonableness if it is on standard forms or in an inter-business dealing *Watford Electronics v Sanderson*
Under the Unfair Terms in Consumer Contracts Regulations a term must not be an unfair surprise or be contrary to good faith *Director General of Fair Trading v First National Bank plc*

4.1 Representations

Bissett v Wilkinson **[1927] AC 177**

A vendor sold land in New Zealand to a purchaser who wished to use it for sheep farming, although it had not been used for that purpose. The vendor, when asked by the purchaser, roughly estimated that the land could support 2,000 sheep, although it was actually impractical for sheep farming. The purchaser sued.

The court held that, because of the inexperience of the vendor, the representation was merely an honest opinion, and not actionable since no reliance could be placed on it.

Esso Petroleum Co Ltd v Marden **[1976] QB 801**

Esso built a petrol station and represented to Marden, the intended franchisee, that it would have a throughput of 200,000 gallons per year. The Local Authority refused planning permission for the layout so the pumps had no access from the main road, only from side roads. Sales only reached 78,000 gallons and Marden could not repay a loan from Esso who sued for repossession.

Esso argued unsuccessfully that the statement on likely throughput was a mere opinion. This failed because of Esso's extensive expertise in the area. The court held that Marden was able to rely on the estimate as though it was a factual statement, albeit inaccurate, and thus a negligently made misrepresentation.

Lord Denning said 'If a man, who has or professes to have special knowledge or skill, makes a representation … to another … with the intention of inducing him to enter into a contract … he is under a duty to use reasonable care to see that the representation is correct … If he negligently gives unsound advice or misleading information or expresses an erroneous opinion, and thereby induces the other side into a contract with him, he is liable'.

4.2 Terms

4.2.1 Incorporating express terms into the contract

CA *Oscar Chess Ltd v Williams* **[1957] 1 WLR 370**

A motorist sold his car to the claimant motor dealers for £290, describing it as a 1948 Morris 10, honestly believing that this was correct as it was the age given in the registration documents. It was later found to be a 1939 model and the motor dealers sued as the value of the car was inevitably lower than they had paid.

The action failed as the defendant had no specialist skill, and was reliant on the registration documents in making the statement. The court held that it was merely an innocent misrepresentation.

Prior to the Misrepresentation Act 1967, there was no remedy available except in equity, so it was vital for the claimant to prove that the statement was incorporated as a term of the contract.

CA **_Routledge v McKay_ [1954] 1 WLR 615**

Registration documents wrongly stated the age of a motorcycle. The owner, unaware of this, gave this age to the claimant. The claimant bought the motorcycle a week later in a written contract with the age not stated and sued unsuccessfully.

The court held the lapse of time too wide for a binding relationship based on the statement which was not incorporated into the contract. Since the written agreement made no mention of age the court held that it was not important enough to be a term.

KBDC **_L'Estrange v Graucob_ [1934] 2 KB 394**

The claimant bought a vending machine from the defendants on a written contract which contained an exclusion of liability for the implied terms in the Sale of Goods Act 1893, then permissible. The machine was defective and the claimant sued unsuccessfully for breach of the implied term of fitness for purpose in the Act.

The court held that the claimant was bound by the express terms of the contract which she had accepted with her signature.

Scrutton LJ stated 'When a document containing contractual terms is signed ... in the absence of fraud, or ... misrepresentation, the party signing it is bound, and it is wholly immaterial whether he has read the document or not'.

The rule seems to be unjust and lacks firm theoretical foundation. It would now be subject to the Unfair Contract Terms Act and Unfair Terms in Consumer Contracts Regulations.

4.2.2 The 'parol evidence rule'

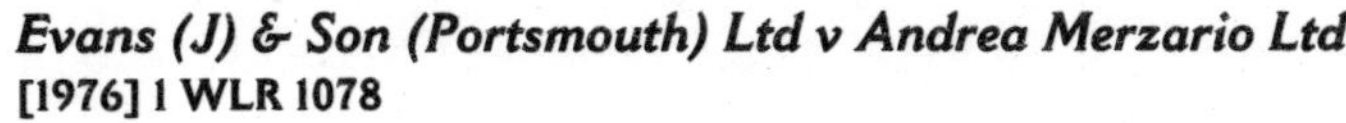

CA **_Evans (J) & Son (Portsmouth) Ltd v Andrea Merzario Ltd_**
[1976] 1 WLR 1078

The claimant regularly used the defendant carrier to ship machinery from Italy and did so on the defendants' standard forms. Originally the machines were always carried below decks because to avoid rusting. The defendant then started using containers, which were generally kept on deck. The claimant raised concerns about rusting and was given oral assurance that its machinery would still be stored below decks. One of the claimant's machines was put in a container and by error stored on deck. It was not properly secured and fell overboard. The claimant sued and won.

The court held that the oral assurance could be introduced as evidence. The standard forms did not represent the actual agreement, and the defendant was liable.

4.2.3 Terms implied by fact

Exch *Hutton v Warren* **[1836] 150 ER 517**

By long standing local custom, tenants were given allowances for seed and labour on termination of agricultural leases. This was important then because most people were engaged in subsistence agriculture. The claimant succeeded in enforcing the custom.

The court held that the lease must be viewed in the light of the custom which was an implied term and was binding.

Parke J said 'in commercial transactions extrinsic evidence of custom and usage is admissible to annex incidents to written contracts, in matters with respect to which they are silent'.

HL *Schawel v Reade* **[1913] 2 IR 64**

The claimant wished to buy a stallion for stud purposes and was examining one advertised for sale at the defendant's stables. The defendant said 'You need not look for anything: the horse is perfectly sound. If there was anything the matter with the horse I would tell you'. The claimant halted his inspection and bought the horse which was unfit for stud purposes. He succeeded in his claim.

The court held that, while the defendant's statement was not an express warranty as to the horse's fitness for stud, it was still an implied warranty that the claimant could rely on. By implication the assurance covered any purpose for which the horse was bought.

 ***Moorcock (The)*** **(1889) 14 PD 64**

The defendant owned a wharf and jetty on the Thames and contracted with the claimant for him to dock his ship and unload cargo there. Both parties knew at the time of contracting that this could involve the ship being at the jetty at low tide. The ship was in fact too big for the depth of water at low tide and became grounded and broke up on a ridge of rock. The claimant sued successfully.

The court held that the defendant gave an implied undertaking that the ship would not be damaged. Without this the whole purpose of the contract would be defeated. The defendant was liable.

Bowen LJ explained 'In business transactions such as this, what the law desires to effect by the implication is to give such business efficacy … as must have been intended at all events by both parties who are businessmen'.

 ***Shell (UK) Ltd v Lostock Garage Ltd*** **[1977] 1 All ER 481**

Shell contracted to supply petrol to Lostock with an undertaking that Lostock would buy it only from Shell. During a 'price-war' Shell supplied petrol to other garages at lower prices causing Lostock to sell at a loss. Lostock unsuccessfully argued for an implied term that Shell would not 'abnormally discriminate' against it.

The court rejected the argument since implied terms depend on the presumed intention of both parties and Shell would not have agreed to such a term.

4.2.4 Terms implied by common law

HL ***Liverpool City Council v Irwin*** **[1976] 2 WLR 562**

The council leased flats in a tower block with no proper tenancy agreement although there was a list of tenants' duties signed by the tenants. The council had no express duties in the agreement. It failed to maintain common areas such as the stairs, lifts, corridors and rubbish chutes which became badly vandalised over time. Tenants withheld their rent in protest and the council sued for repossession. The claimants counterclaimed arguing a breach of an implied term that the council should maintain the common areas.

In the Court of Appeal Lord Denning felt that such a term could be implied as it was reasonable in the circumstances. The House of Lords rejected this approach and did not accept that the council had any absolute duty to maintain the common areas. It did, however, accept that there was an implied term to take reasonable care to maintain the common areas but this had not been breached.

Lord Wilberforce said that to follow Lord Denning's approach would 'extend a long, and undesirable, way beyond sound authority'. **Lord Cross** stated that the 'officious bystander test is the appropriate method for terms to be implied into a contract'.

Paragon Finance v Nash **[2001] EWCA Civ 1466**

Mortgage lenders made loans on variable interest rates thus giving them discretion to raise or lower the rates. The claimants fell into arrears and tried to challenge the agreements on the basis that the lender's interest rates were much higher than rates of other lenders.

The court held that a term should be implied into such contracts that rates should not be set arbitrarily or for any improper purpose to prevent defendants from exercising the discretion to set rates 'unreasonably', under to the *Wednesbury* principle. The rate should not be set so that no other mortgage lender, acting in a reasonable way, would do. However, the loan agreement was not excessive even though it did not follow the bank rate or other lenders, nor was it unlawful under the Consumer Credit Act 1974 or the Unfair Contract Terms Act 1977 so the implied term was not breached.

4.2.5 Terms implied by statute

Rowland v Divall **[1923] 2 KB 500**

The claimant bought a car which he then discovered to be stolen. The rightful owner succeeded in claiming the full price of the car.

The court, applying s 12 Sale of Goods Act 1979, held that the seller had no rights of ownership and owed the value to the rightful owner.

Moore & Co. and Landauer & Co's Arbitration (Re)
[1921] 2 KB 519

In a contract for sale and purchase of a consignment of tinned fruit delivery was to be in cartons of 30 tins. On delivery half of the cartons were of 24 tins. The purchaser refused to accept them.

The court held that there was a breach of s 13, the implied term that goods must correspond with their description, even though the quantity of tins ordered was correct and the buyer intended to sell them on so would have been unaffected by the breach.

The court took a very narrow view of description here.

Kendall (Henry) & Sons v William Lillico & Sons Ltd
[1969] 2 AC 31

The claimant bought groundnut extract, normally used as cattle food, and used it to feed game birds that he bred. The groundnut contained a toxin that killed many of the birds and the buyer sued.

The court rejected the claim under s 14(2) since the goods were 'merchantable'. They were fit for their normal purposes.

The word 'merchantable' had the potential for unjust results. As a result an amending Act has changed the word to 'satisfactory'.

HL **_Grant v Australian Knitting Mills Ltd_ [1936] AC 85**

The claimant bought woollen underpants which contained traces of chemicals causing him a painful skin disease and sued.

The court held that underpants have a single purpose which the buyer impliedly made known as the purpose for which he bought them even if he did not actually state it to the seller. There was a clear breach of the implied term. They were not fit for this purpose.

QBD **_Godley v Perry_ [1960] 1 WLR 9 QBD**

A boy suffered injury to an eye when the elastic on a catapult that he had bought snapped. The retailer had been supplied after seeing a sample of the toy. He had tested this sample and sued the supplier.

The supplier was liable as the bulk of the goods, including this catapult, did not match the quality of the sample so the supplier had breached the implied term in s 15 Sale of Goods Act 1979.

4.2.6 The relative significance of terms

Poussard v Spiers and Pond **(1876) 1 QBD 410**

An actress contracted to appear as the lead singer in an operetta for a season. She was taken ill and could not attend the early performances. The producers gave her role to the understudy and she sued unsuccessfully for breach of contract.

The court held that she had breached her contract by being late for the first night. As the lead singer her presence was crucial to the production and was a condition entitling the producers to repudiate.

QBD ***Bettini v Gye*** **[1876] 1 QBD 183**

A singer contracted to appear in different theatres for a season of concerts. The contract included a term that he should attend rehearsals for six days before beginning the actual performances. He was absent for the first three days of rehearsals and on returning his role had been replaced. He sued and the producers' claim that the obligation to attend rehearsals was a condition failed.

The court held that the requirement was only ancillary to the main purpose of the contract, appearing in the actual production. The breach entitled the producers to sue for damages but not to repudiate which they had therefore done unlawfully.

4.2.7 How judges construe terms

HL

Schuler (L.) AG v Wickman Machine Tool Sales Ltd **[1974] AC 235**

Wickman was appointed sole distributor of Schuler's presses. In a condition in the contract Wickman's representatives were to make weekly visits to six large UK motor manufacturers and solicit orders for presses. Another condition stated that the contract could be terminated for breach of any condition that was not remedied within 60 days. The contract was for four years, amounting to more than 1,400 visits. Some way into the contract Wickman's representatives failed to make a visit and Schuler sought to terminate the contract.

The court held that it was inevitable that during the length of the contract sometimes maintaining weekly visits would be impossible. If the term was a condition this would entitle Schuler to terminate the contract even for one failure to visit out of the 1,400. This would be an unreasonable burden so the term could not be a condition.

Cehave NV v Bremer Handelsgesselschaft mbH (The Hansa Nord) **[1976] QB 44**

A cargo of citrus pulp pellets for use as cattle feed was rejected by the buyer as part had overheated, breaching a term of the contract 'Shipment to be made in good condition'. The seller would not refund the price already paid so the buyer applied to a Rotterdam court which ordered its sale. Another party bought the cargo and sold it to the original buyer at a lower price than the original price. It still used the cargo as cattle feed but argued that the goods breached the implied condition of merchantable quality under the Sale of Goods Act, justifying its repudiation.

It succeeded at first instance but the Court of Appeal applied the *Hong Kong Fir* approach, holding that, as the goods were used for their original purpose, there was no breach serious enough to justify repudiation. Only an action for damages was appropriate.

Hong Kong Fir Shipping Co Ltd v Kawasaki Kisen Kaisha Ltd [1962] 2 QB 26.

HL ***Reardon Smith Line Ltd v Hansen-Tangen* [1976] 1 WLR 989**

A contract for a tanker described it as 'Osaka 354', a shipyard number. Because the shipyard had too many orders the work was sub-contracted to another yard and the job was described as 'Oshima 004'. The need for tankers lessened and the buyers tried to avoid the contract, claiming breach of a condition that the tanker should correspond with the full description in the documentation.

The court held that since the breach was entirely technical with no bearing on the outcome it could not justify repudiation.

4.3 Judicial and statutory control of exclusion clauses

4.3.1 Incorporation of exclusion clauses

CA ***Olley v Marlborough Court Hotel*** **[1949] 1 KB 532**

The claimant booked into the hotel at which point the contract was formed. She then went out and left the key at reception as required by the hotel rules. In her absence a third party took the key, entered her room and stole her fur coat. She sought compensation from the hotel owner who tried to rely on an exclusion clause: 'the proprietors will not hold themselves liable for articles lost or stolen unless handed to the manageress for safe custody'. Mrs Olley sued.

The court held that the clause had not been incorporated into the contract as it was on a notice on a wall inside the hotel room. When the contract was formed the claimant was unaware of the clause.

McCutcheon v David MacBrayne Ltd **[1964] 1 WLR 125**

The claimant had used the defendants' ferries to ship his car from Islay to the Scottish mainland on many occasions. Sometimes he was asked to sign a risk note including an exclusion clause and on other occasions he was not. On this occasion the claimant's relative took the car to the ferry and was not asked to sign a risk note. The ferry sank through the defendants' negligence and the car was destroyed. The claimant sued for compensation and the defendants then tried to rely on the exclusion clause in the risk note.

The court held that the defendant could not rely on the exclusion and the action must fail because there was no consistent course of action that allowed them to assume that the claimant knew of its exclusion clause so it was not incorporated in the contract.

Lord Devlin said: 'previous dealings are only relevant if they prove knowledge of the terms actual ... not constructive and assent to them'.

Spurling (J.) Ltd v Bradshaw [1956] 1 WLR 561.

4.3.2 Construction of the contract

CA ***Chapelton v Barry Urban District Council*** **[1940] 1 KB 532**

The claimant hired deckchairs on the beach at Barry, receiving two tickets from the council's beach attendant on paying for them. On the back of the small tickets was written 'The council will not be liable for any accident or damage arising from the hire of the chair'. The claimant did not read this, thinking it was a mere receipt. One chair was defective and collapsed, injuring him, and he sued for compensation. The council tried to rely on its exclusion clause.

The court held that the clause was not lawful since its existence was not effectively bought to the claimant's attention. To assume that the claimant would understand that the ticket was contractual was unreasonable and the council was liable.

Exclusion clauses are not incorporated into contracts if, on objective analysis, they are not in a form that would be seen as contractual.

Parker v South Eastern Railway Co. (1877) 2 CPD 416.

CA ***Thornton v Shoe Lane Parking Ltd***
[1971] 2 QB 163

The claimant was injured in the defendants' car park. A notice at the entrance identified the charges, and stated that parking was at the owner's risk. On entering motorists had to stop at a barrier and take a ticket from a machine, then the barrier would lift, allowing entry. On each ticket were the words 'issued subject to the conditions of issue as displayed on the premises'. Notices inside the car park listed these, including an exclusion for property damage and personal injury. The claimant sued successfully for his injuries.

The defendant tried to rely on the exclusion clause but the court rejected this and held that there was insufficient attempt made to draw the claimant's attention to the existence of the clause for the defendant to be able to rely on it to avoid liability.

Lord Denning said the customer 'pays his money and gets a ticket. He cannot refuse it. He cannot get his money back. He may protest to the

> machine, even swear at it. But it will remain unmoved. He is committed beyond recall ... The contract was concluded at that time'. The customer is bound by the terms of the contract 'as long as they are sufficiently bought to his notice before-hand, but not otherwise'. He repeated his words from *Spurling v Bradshaw*: 'Some clauses ... need to be printed in red ink with a red hand pointing to them before the notice could be held to be sufficient'.

4.3.3 Other limitations on the use of exclusion clauses

Curtis v Chemical Cleaning and Dyeing Co. Ltd
[1951] 1 KB 805

The claimant took a wedding dress for cleaning and was asked to sign a document containing a clause exempting the defendants from liability for any damage 'howsoever arising'. She queried this and the sales assistant assured her that it referred only to damage to beads or sequins attached to items. The dress was ruined by chemical stains and she claimed successfully.

The court held that the defendant could not rely on the exclusion clause which was overridden by the oral assurances.

A party is usually bound by a contract that he has signed but an oral misrepresentation makes an exclusion clause ineffective because it is the misrepresentation that induces the other party to contract.

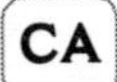

Hollier v Rambler Motors (AMC) Ltd [1972] QB 71

The claimant took his car to a garage for repair as he had often done before. The normal conditions of the contract were in a form that he had signed on previous occasions. This form included a term that 'The company is not responsible for damage caused by fire to customers' cars on the premises'. The car was damaged in a fire caused by the defendants' negligence and the owner sued for compensation. The garage owner tried to rely on the clause.

The court held that the term could not be incorporated just because of previous dealings and that to rely on the exclusion clause it must have stated without any ambiguity that it would not be liable for its own negligence. In the absence of such precise wording the customer might rightly conclude when making the contract that the garage owners would not generally be liable, except where the fire damage was caused by their own negligence when they would be.

Photo Productions Ltd v Securicor Transport Ltd [1980] AC 827

Securicor contracted on its standard terms to provide night patrols at the claimant's factory. A clause in its standard terms stated that it would in no circumstances 'be responsible for any injurious act or default by any employee of the company unless such act or default could have been foreseen and avoided by … due diligence [by the] Company'. The security officer started a fire that burnt down a large part of the factory. It was not disputed whether the guard was suitable nor was Securicor was negligent in employing him.

The trial judge held that the exclusion clause applied. The Court of Appeal applied the doctrine of fundamental breach and held that the whole contract was effectively breached so that Securicor could not rely on its exclusion clause. The House of Lords reversed this decision and affirmed that parties dealing in free negotiations are entitled to include in their contracts any exclusion, limitation or modification to their obligations that they choose by which both parties are bound. As the clause was clear and unambiguous there was nothing to prevent its use and it protected Securicor from liability for its employee's actions. The judgments also criticised the use of the doctrine of fundamental breach.

Lord Diplock said: 'In cases falling within … fundamental breach, the anticipatory secondary obligation [to pay damages] arises … by implication of the common law, except to the extent that it is excluded or modified by the express words of the contract'.

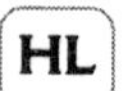

Ailsa Craig Fishing Co. Ltd v Malvern Fishing Co. Ltd
[1983] 1 WLR 964

Securicor contracted with the Aberdeen Fishing Vessels Owners Association, which acted for fishing boat owners, to provide security in a harbour. Following negligence by a security guard one vessel fouled another; both sank and got trapped under the quay. The contract was on Securicor's standard terms and when sued it tried to rely on a term limiting liability 'for any loss or damage of whatever nature arising out of or connected with the provision of or failure in provision of, the services covered by this contract … to a sum … not exceeding £1,000 [for] one claim … and … £10,000 for the consequences of any incident involving fire, theft or any other cause', sums that were small compared to the likely cost of damage.

The House rejected the argument that since Securicor clearly failed to carry out the terms of its contract it should be unable to rely on the limitation clause. The House stated that limitation clauses should not to be regarded with the same hostility as exclusion clauses because they relate to the risks to which the defending party is exposed, the remuneration he may receive and the opportunity the other party has to insure against loss. It held that the clause was drafted sufficiently clearly and unambiguously to protect Securicor. Besides this the two parties were commercial enterprises and had contracted freely and with equal bargaining strength. (The contract was made before the Unfair Contract Terms Act otherwise the result may have been different.)

Lord Wilberforce said the court 'must not strive to create ambiguities by strained construction … The relevant words must be given, if possible, their natural, plain meaning'.

These so-called 'Securicor cases' suggest that the doctrine of fundamental breach no longer applies, and, subject now to statutory controls, when parties of equal bargaining strength freely negotiate they can include even very onerous terms which bind them both.

4.3.4 The Unfair Contract Terms Act 1977

Watford Electronics Ltd v Sanderson CFL
[2001] 1 All ER (Comm.) 696

The defendant provided and integrated software into the claimant's existing computer system for £105,000. He then terminated the agreement because the system did not work satisfactorily and sued for damages for breach of contract for £5.5 million, or for misrepresentation and negligence of £1.1 million. In the defendant's standard terms a clause excluded liability for any claims for indirect or consequential losses arising from negligence or otherwise and limiting liability to the price of the goods supplied.

The court held that the Act applied to the contract so the question was whether the clause satisfied the test of reasonableness. It held that it did since the parties were of equal bargaining power and the limitation clause had been subject to negotiation.

***George Mitchell Ltd v Finney Lock Seeds Ltd* [1983] 2 AC 803**

Seed merchants supplied farmers with Dutch winter cabbage seed for £192. A limitation clause in the contract limited their liability in the event of breach to the cost of the seed only or to replacement seed. The farmers sowed 63 acres with the seed, calculating their profit at £61,000. The seed was the wrong sort and there was no crop. The farmers sued successfully for their lost profit.

The supplier argued that it was protected by the limitation clause. The Court of Appeal held that the clause was not sufficiently clear or unambiguous for the supplier to rely on it to exclude liability for breaches of implied terms in the Sale of Goods Act 1979. The House of Lords held that, on proper construction of the clause, it did cover the breach, but, using the terminology in the Unfair Contract Terms Act, it was unreasonable and could not be relied on. The supplier had settled out of court before and could have insured against the likely loss without altering its profits substantially.

Overland Shoes Ltd v Shenkers Ltd **[1998] 1 Lloyd's Rep 498**

Overland imported shoes and Shenkers, international freight carriers, contracted to transport them. The contract was on the standard forms of the British International Freight Association, including a 'no set off' clause. When Shenkers claimed for their freight charges Overland tried to set off against these sums that Shenkers owed for VAT. Shenkers objected pointing to the 'no set off' clause. Overland argued that this was in effect an exclusion clause and was unreasonable under the test in the Act.

The court held that the clause satisfied the test of reasonableness in the Act as it was based on long-standing established custom.

4.3.5 The Unfair Terms in Consumer Contracts Regulations 1999

Director General of Fair Trading v First National Bank plc
[2002] 1 All ER 97

In a standard clause in a loan agreement if a lender defaulted on an instalment of the loan from a bank the full amount became payable. A connected clause identified that interest on the outstanding debt would be payable even following any court judgment. The Director General, using the regulations, challenged this clause.

The Court of Appeal held that this was an 'unfair surprise' contrary to the 'good faith' requirement in regulation 4(1) (5(1) in the 1999 regulations). The House of Lords disagreed and held that the words 'significant imbalance' in the regulation referred to the substance of the agreement but 'good faith' covered only procedural fairness and the clause did not contravene the regulations. Lord Steyn thought the words should cover both, in other words not just the fairness of the making of the contract but also of the terms contained in it.

CHAPTER 5

VITIATING FACTORS

Misrepresentation:
A misrepresentation is a false statement of material facts used to induce a party to enter a contract *Edgington v Fitzmaurice*
3 classes:
Fraudulent – made knowingly, without belief in or recklessly *Derry v Peek*
Negligent – in tort where there is a special relationship and it is reasonable for a party to rely on the advice *Hedley Byrne v Heller & Partners*
Or under s 2(1) Misrepresentation Act 1967 *Howard Marine Dredging Co. Ltd v A Ogden & Sons (Excavating) Ltd*
A contract formed because of a misrepresentation can also be rescinded in equity *Redgrave v Hurd*

Mistake:
Common mistake – where both parties mistake the existence of the subject-matter the contract is void *Couturier v Hastie*
But a common mistake as to quality has no effect on the contract *Bell v Lever Bros*
Mutual mistake – where the parties are at cross purposes the contract may be void *Raffles v Wichelhaus*
Unilateral mistake – where one party is mistaken and the other knows of the mistake the contract is void *Cundy v Lindsay*
In face-to-face dealings the party is presumed to deal with the person in front of him *Lewis v Avery*

Vitiating factors

Duress and undue influence:
Duress:
A contract can be avoided where it is made as a result of threats of violence *Barton v Armstrong*
Economic duress:
This applies also where a party is put under excess commercial pressure *Atlas Express v Kafco*
Undue influence:
Traditionally a person in a special relationship could avoid a contract made through this unfair influence *Allcard v Skinner*
Otherwise the unfair pressure must be proved *National Westminster Bank v Morgan*
Now there are detailed rules *Royal Bank of Scotland plc v Etridge (No 2)*

Illegality:
Some contracts are prohibited by statute *Cope v Rowlands*
Restraint of trade clauses in employment contracts are *prima facie* void unless they protect a legitimate interest and are reasonable *Herbert Morris Ltd v Saxelby*
This applies also to vendor restraints *Nordenfelt v Maxim Nordenfelt Co,*
If it is possible part of the clause may be severed *Attwood v Lamont*
Common law also makes immoral contracts unenforceable *Pearce v Brooks*
And those based on corruption *Parkinson v College of Ambulance*

5.1 Misrepresentation

5.1.1 'Misrepresentation' defined

Edgington v Fitzmaurice **(1885) 29 Ch D 459**

Company directors borrowed money, representing that the loan was to be used for improvements to company buildings when in fact they meant to use it to pay off serious debts owed by the company.

The court held that the directors had misrepresented their actual intentions. This amounted to a false statement of material fact and was an actionable misrepresentation.

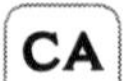

Peyman v Lanjani **[1985] 2 WLR 154**

The defendant, who spoke no English, arranged with another man to impersonate him to gain a lease from the landlord. When he wished to assign the lease to the claimant he again sent the other man to impersonate him to get the landlord's permission for the assignment. The claimant found out when he had paid £10,000 for the assignment and successfully sought rescission.

The court held that the impersonation was a misrepresentation of the legitimacy of the lease which in fact had never been agreed between the defendant and the landlord.

Museprime Properties Ltd v Adhill Properties Ltd [1990] EGLR 196

Prior to three properties being sold by auction a false representation was made concerning the existence of an outstanding rent review which could result in increased rents and therefore increased revenue, making it a more attractive proposition. The defendants unsuccessfully challenged the claimants' action for rescission.

The court rejected the defence that the statement could realistically induce nobody to enter the contract and applied a subjective test. It was unimportant whether a reasonable bidder would have been induced by the representation the question was merely whether or not the claimant was induced by it to enter the contract.

Spice Girls Ltd v Aprilia World Service BV [2000] EMLR 478

A girl group was offered a contract with scooter manufacturers to promote its products. Before signing the contract they filmed a commercial despite all knowing that one of them planned to leave.

The court held that the presence of all members of the group at the filming of the commercial amounted to a representation that none of them intended to leave the group and none of them was aware that one member intended to. As such it was a false statement of fact made by their conduct in attending and misrepresentation.

5.1.2 Classes of misrepresentation and their remedies

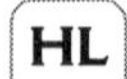

Derry v Peek **(1889) 14 App Cas 337**

The defendant was licensed to operate horse-drawn trams by Act of Parliament. It was also possible under the Act to use mechanical power with the certification of the Board of Trade. The defendant applied for a licence and issued a prospectus to raise further share capital. In this it falsely represented that it could use mechanical power, honestly believing the licence would be granted. However, its application was denied and it fell into liquidation. The claimant invested on the strength of the representation and lost money as a result of the liquidation, and sued in the tort of deceit but failed.

There was insufficient proof of fraud. Lord Herschell held that what was needed was actual proof that the false representation was made 'knowingly or without belief in its truth or recklessly careless whether it be true or false'.

Smith New Court Securities v Scrimgeour Vickers **[1996] 4 All ER 769**

The claimant was induced to buy shares at 82.25p per share as a result of a fraudulent misrepresentation that the company was a good marketing risk. The shares were trading at 78p at the time of the transaction. Unknown to either party, the shares were worth far less as the defendant had been the victim of a major fraud. The claimant chose not to rescind on discovering the fraud but sold the shares at prices ranging from 49p to 30p per share and sued.

The court held that the claimant's loss was a direct result of the fraud that had induced them to contract and that damages awarded should be based on the figure actually paid of 82.25p rather than the actual value of the shares at the time purchased, 78p.

The judgment is significant because it means heavier claims can be pursued if fraud is alleged and can be proved.

HL ***Hedley Byrne & Co. Ltd v Heller & Partners Ltd***
[1964] AC 465

The claimant was asked to provide advertising worth £100,000 on credit for a small company, Easipower. It sought a credit reference from Easipower's bankers, who confirmed that Easipower was a 'respectably constituted company good for … ordinary business' but included a disclaimer of liability for this advice. Easipower went into liquidation. The claimant was still unpaid and sued the bank in negligence but failed because of the valid disclaimer.

The House, *in obiter*, approved Lord Denning's dissenting judgment in *Candler v Crane, Christmas & Co.* (1951), and considered that the action would be possible in certain 'special relationships' where the person making the negligent statement owed a duty of care to the other party to ensure that the statement was accurately made. It was not clear on what would constitute such a special relationship.

Later case law has accepted and refined the *Hedley Byrne* principle. Originally there were three requirements:

- The party negligently making the false statement must possess the particular type of knowledge required for the advice.
- There must be sufficient proximity between the two parties that it is reasonable to rely on the statement.
- The party to whom the statement is made does in fact rely on the statement and the party making it is aware of that reliance.

Later case law has added further requirements:

- The party negligently making the statement must have known the reasons why the claimant needed the advice.
- The party negligently making the statement must have assumed responsibility to give advice in the circumstances.

***Howard Marine Dredging Co. Ltd v A Ogden & Sons (Excavating) Ltd* [1978] QB 574**

The claimant, in estimating a price for depositing excavated earth at sea, asked advice from the company it meant to hire barges from as to their exact capacity of the barges. The advice was negligently based on dead weight figures from Lloyd's Register rather than the actual shipping register. Delays resulted in the work as a result of the differences in capacity and the claimant refused to pay the hire charge. When sued for payment it successfully counterclaimed using s 2(1) of the Misrepresentation Act 1967.

The court held that there was insufficient evidence to support the defendant's argument that the advice was based on an honest belief in the figure given. No attempt had been made to check the correct figure on the actual shipping register.

CA **Royscot Trust Ltd v Rogerson** [1991] 3 All ER 294

A car dealer sold a car on a loan financed by hire purchase. In the hire purchase agreement the dealer misrepresented to the finance company the deposit made. The purchaser defaulted on the loan and sold the car to an innocent third party who gained good title to the car under the Hire Purchase Act 1964. The finance company suffered loss and successfully sued under the Misrepresentation Act 1967 by showing that it would not have lent as much to the purchaser if it had known the true deposit.

The court confirmed that the measure of damages under s 2(1) of the Misrepresentation Act 1967 is tortious rather than contractual. Also because the wording of the section states that the action is in place of one in fraud, where damages would have been awarded if fraud could be proved, then the damages should be the same as in the tort of deceit.

This means that the claimant can recover for all damages that are a consequence of the misrepresentation rather than just those that are a reasonably foreseeable loss. Another consequence is that they can also be reduced for contributory negligence.

5.1.3 Equity and misrepresentation

Redgrave v Hurd **(1881) 20 Ch D 1**

A solicitor selling his practice misstated its income and when the purchaser backed out on learning of this the seller tried to claim specific performance of the contract. The other solicitor successfully counterclaimed for rescission for misrepresentation.

There was no action possible at the time so equity intervened.

Sir George Jessell explained: 'no man ought to seek to take advantage of his own false statements'.

5.1.4 Non-disclosure amounting to misrepresentation

Locker and Woolf Ltd v Western Australian Insurance Co. Ltd **[1936] 1 KB 408**

The defendant had not revealed to an insurer on entering a contract that another company had refused him insurance.

The court held that, while non-disclosure usually cannot amount to misrepresentation, it may do where the relationship is *uberrimae fidei* (of the utmost good faith). The information was clearly material to the contract and failure to give it was misrepresentation.

Fletcher v Krell (1873) 42 LJ QB 55.

5.2 Mistake

5.2.1 The classes of mistake

HL ***Couturier v Hastie*** **(1852) 5 HLC 673**

In a contract for sale and purchase of a cargo of grain in transit, that both parties believed existed at the time of the contract, the captain of the ship had sold the cargo, as was customary practice, when it had begun to overheat. The buyer sued unsuccessfully.

The court declared the contract void. It rejected the seller's argument that the buyer had accepted the risk.

Coleridge J made did not mention mistake but held that since the subject-matter of the contract did not exist at the time of contracting then neither did the contract. This rule is now in s 6 Sale of Goods Act 1979. Alternatively common mistake, *res extincta* applies (the subject-matter did not exist at the time of the contract, unknown to either party).

HL ***Cooper v Phibbs*** **(1867) LR 2 HL 149**

Cooper took a three-year lease for a salmon fishery from Phibbs, both believing that Phibbs owned it. Cooper was then found to be the life tenant. He could not dispose of the property but was effective owner when contracting. He sought to set the lease aside.

The House allowed this but granted Phibbs a lien in respect of the considerable expense he had gone to in improving the property.

The case was decided on equitable principles but is accepted as an example of *res sua* (subject-matter in different ownership).

HL **_Bell v Lever Brothers Ltd_ [1932] AC 161**

Lever Brothers employed Bell as Chairman of its subsidiary company to rejuvenate it, which he successfully did. The subsidiary was then merged with another and Lever agreed a settlement of £30,000 for the termination of Bell's contract. It then discovered that Bell was in breach of a clause in his contract, prohibiting private dealings and sued unsuccessfully for return of the settlement.

The House of Lords held that there was no common mistake which would void the contract because the mistake was not operative. It was not the reason why Lever agreed the settlement. This was to reward Bell for the early termination of a completed contract.

Lord Atkin said: 'In such a case, a mistake will not affect assent unless it is the mistake of both parties and is as to the existence of some quality which makes the thing without the quality essentially different from the thing as it was believed to be'.

Lord Atkin accepted that a sufficiently fundamental mistake as to quality of the subject-matter can void a contract but refused to find this contract void. It has been argued that it is hard to imagine a more fundamental mistake and so the standard is set too high.

***Great Peace Shipping Ltd v Tsavliris Salvage (International) Ltd* [2002] EWCA Civ 1407**

The defendant had salvage rights in a ship and, worried that it might sink, approached London brokers who contacted a third party (OR), who identified the nearest vessel, which belonged to the claimant, and the defendant agreed to charter it. A clause in the contract stated that in the event of cancellation the party hiring the vessel still had to pay for a minimum of five days hire. OR was wrong, and the ship was more than 400 miles away so the charter contract was based on a common mistake. The defendant then hired a closer vessel and tried to cancel the contract. The claimant claimed for five days' hire. The defendants argued that the mistake made the contract void at common law or voidable in equity.

The court held that since the mistake was not as to existence of the subject-matter it was not operable and the contract could not be void at common law. Nor could it be set aside in equity because this would amount to making the correctness of the information given by OR a condition of the contract and the parties themselves had included no such condition. Because the vessels were not sufficiently distant that the mistake would make the thing contracted for so essentially different from the thing contracted for, the mistake could not be classed as operative.

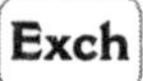

***Raffles v Wichelhaus* [1864] 159 ER 375**

The contract was for the sale of cotton on a ship named *Peerless* sailing out of Bombay. In fact there were two ships named *Peerless* both sailing from Bombay on the same day, with different cargoes. The seller was under the impression that he was selling the cargo other than the one that the buyer was intending to buy.

The court had no way of finding a common intention between the parties and it declared the contract void for mutual mistake.

Pollock CB identified 'parol evidence may be given [to show]that the defendant meant one 'Peerless' and the plaintiff another. [so] there was no *consensus ad idem*, and … no binding contract'.

***Smith v Hughes* (1871) LR 6 QB 597**

Hughes bought oats after examining a sample. On delivery he found that they were 'new oats' rather than the previous year's crop which he wanted. He refused delivery and when the seller sued for the price claimed mistake as he thought he was offered 'good old oats' rather than 'good oats' as the seller claimed.

The court held that it could not declare a contract void merely because one party later discovered it was less advantageous than he believed. The contract stood and Hughes had to pay the price.

Kings Norton Metal Co. Ltd v Edridge, Merrett & Co. Ltd (The Kings Norton Metal Case) **(1897) 14 TLR 98**

A rogue contracted under a fictitious name to purchase expensive items which were supplied but never paid for. The claimant sued to recover them from the party who purchased them from the rogue.

The court would not void the contract for mistake. The mistake was not the identity but the creditworthiness of the rogue.

Cundy v Lindsay **(1878) 3 App Cas 459**

Blenkarn hired a room in Wood Street where a respectable firm, Blenkiron & Co., conducted its business. He ordered handkerchiefs from Lindsay's using a signature designed to be confused with that of the firm. The goods were supplied and billed in the name 'Blenkiron' and not paid for. Blenkarn sold some to Cundy before the fraud was discovered. Lindsay then tried to recover the goods from Cundy.

The House held that the contract was void for mistake. The mistake was operable because the identity of the party trading from Wood Street was material to the formation of the contract. Unlike the *Kings Norton Metal* case, there was a party here with whom the claimants wished to contract and the third party acquired the goods from Blenkarn without any title.

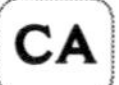

CA ***Lewis v Avery* [1972] 1 QB 198**

A rogue buying a car claimed to be a famous actor of the time and showed the seller a false studio pass when his cheque was at first rejected. The cheque bounced and when the seller saw the car he sued the new owner for recovery but his action failed.

The court held that, while the claimant was induced into believing that the party he contracted with was somebody else, he had still in fact done no more than contract with that party. The mistake was not operative and the contract could not be declared void. In the Court of Appeal Lord Denning suggested that in such cases the mistake would render the contract voidable rather than void. Megaw LJ disagreed. The claimant was not in fact concerned with the true identity of the party with whom he contracted but rather with his creditworthiness, which was not a material mistake.

For a party to claim that the identity of the other party is material to the making of the contract, he must have taken adequate steps to ensure the true identity of the other party.

HL **_Shogun Finance Ltd v Hudson_ [2003] UKHL 62**

A rogue gave a false name (Patel) and address when completing hire-purchase forms to buy a car and showed a false driving licence to confirm his identity. The car dealer faxed a copy to the finance company which checked the credit rating of the real Patel and agreed to finance the purchase. The rogue paid 10% in cash and a cheque and took the car, then sold it to the defendant.

The court applied *nemo dat quod non habet* (a seller cannot pass a title that he does not have). It considered the 'face-to-face' cases but decided that they did not apply. The finance offer was made to the real Patel, not the rogue. The rogue gained no title that he could pass on, and so the innocent purchaser had to bear the loss.

In the Court of Appeal Sedley LJ dissented as he felt that the car dealer acted as agent for the rogue. Certainly a person selling to a rogue is better placed to check his honesty than one who buys from him and the law should protect the more innocent third party.

5.2.2 Mistake and equity

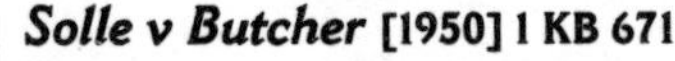

CA **_Solle v Butcher_ [1950] 1 KB 671**

A lease was agreed at one rent, both parties mistaking that the rent was outside statutory control that would have lowered it. The tenant then claimed for a decrease of the rent.

The court held that there was a common mistake over the quality of the contract rather than a mistake as to the existence of the subject-matter so it was not void at common law. It was prepared to set aside the original terms that were unworkable.

Great Peace Shipping Ltd v Tsavliris Salvage (International) Ltd [2002] EWCA Civ 1407 (p83) which says that equity cannot apply in common mistake.

Webster v Cecil **[1861] 54 ER 812**

A written contract for sale of land showed the price at £1,250 but letters showed that an offer of £2,000 had already been rejected. An action for specific performance of the written agreement failed.

The court held the claim must fail since the written agreement was clearly inconsistent with the agreement actually reached.

5.2.3 *Non est factum*

HL ***Saunders v Anglian Building Society*** **[1970] AC 1004**

An elderly widow decided to transfer property to her nephew, provided she could live there for the rest of her life. She did this so the nephew could borrow money to start a business. The document was drafted by Lee, a dishonest friend of the nephew, and was a conveyance to him rather than a deed of gift to the nephew. Lee then borrowed against the property and defaulted on the loan.

The widow, in a claim for repossession, pleaded *non est factum* (this is not my deed). The House rejected this as there was insufficient difference between the document she signed and that she intended to sign and she had not done enough to check its nature.

5.3 Duress, economic duress and undue influence

5.3.1 Duress

PC ***Barton v Armstrong*** **[1975] 2 All ER 465**

A former chairman of a company threatened to kill the current managing director unless he paid over a large sum of money for the former chairman's shares. It was shown in the case that the managing director was actually quite happy to buy the shares and would have done so even without the threat.

Nevertheless threats had been made and the court held that these were enough to amount to duress, vitiating the agreement they had reached. The agreement was set aside for duress.

HL ***Williams v Bayley*** **(1886) LR 1 HL 200**

A young man had forged endorsements [signatures] on promissory notes (IOUs) and caused a bank to lose money as a result. The bank approached his father, demanding that the father mortgage his farm to the bank to cover the son's debt to them.

The court held against the bank because of the nature of the threats applied to the father. It threatened to prosecute the son unless the father complied and, at that time this would have meant the son's almost certain transportation. The House of Lords held that the pressure was illegitimate and amounted to undue influence, vitiating the agreement and allowing the father to avoid it.

5.3.2 Economic duress

Occidental Worldwide Investment Corporation v Skibs A/S Avanti (The Siboen and the Sibotre) **[1976] 1 Lloyd's Rep 293**

During a worldwide recession in the shipping industry a charter party demanded renegotiation of its contract with the ship owner, claiming falsely that it would otherwise go out of business and that as it had no assets it was not worth suing. The ship owner had no choice but to agree to the variation. Because of the recession it would have had little chance of other charters of its vessels.

The court held that the question was whether there was 'such a degree of coercion that the other party was deprived of his free consent and agreement'. Other factors included: whether the party protested immediately; and accepted the agreement or tried to argue openly.

Lord Scarman said it was possible to recognise 'economic duress as a factor which may render a contract voidable provided always that the basis of such recognition is that it must always amount to a coercion of will which vitiates consent'. **Lord Kerr** said the basic question is 'was there such a degree of coercion that the other party was deprived of his free consent and agreement'.

Atlas Express Ltd v Kafco (Importers and Distributors) Ltd
[1989] QB 833

The claimant, a carrier, contracted to deliver the defendant's basketwork to retailers. Each delivery was estimated at between 400 and 600 cartons and a price of £1.10p per carton agreed. In fact loads only amounted to about 200 cartons each and the claimant refused to carry any more without a minimum of £440 per load. The defendant had no alternative transport and was forced to agree to the demand to protect its contract with retailers. It then failed to pay the agreed new rate and the claimant sued.

The court held that the claimant was coerced by economic duress and the claimant was unable to enforce the new agreement.

Tucker J said 'the defendant's apparent consent to the agreement was induced by pressure which was illegitimate [and] can properly be described as economic duress … a concept recognised by English law, and which … vitiates the defendant's … consent'.

North Ocean Shipping Co. Ltd v Hyundai Construction Co. Ltd (The Atlantic Baron) [1978] QB 705

A shipyard contracted to build a tanker for a shipping company to be paid for in five instalments. As part of the contract the shipyard opened a letter of credit for repayment of payments already made if it failed to build the ship. After payment of the first instalment the shipyard demanded a 10% increase in the price. The shipping company reluctantly agreed, as it needed the ship to complete other contracts, and the letter of credit was increased, but many months after the ship was built it sued for return of the excess.

The court accepted that there was economic duress but that the increase in the letter of credit was sufficient consideration for the new promise. It also felt that the long delay before suing indicated that the buyer had affirmed the contract and was bound by it.

If a claimant protests too much at the unfair pressure he runs the risk of a breach, which in *Kafco* would have been disastrous, but if he fails to protest enough then he runs the risk that the court will consider that there has been insufficient protest and fail to declare the contract entered under pressure voidable.

5.3.3 Undue influence

Allcard v Skinner (1887) 36 Ch D 145

A young woman entered a closed religious order, taking vows of poverty and chastity and giving property to the order through the mother superior, her spiritual adviser to whom she owed obedience. After she left the she sued for recovery of the value of property that she had handed over, arguing that the agreement to pass her property was made while she was subjected to undue influence.

The court accepted that, because of the submissive nature of her vows and her duty to obey the mother superior, undue influence could be presumed. She had also never received any independent advice. It would not declare the contract voidable since she waited six years after leaving before suing and 'delay defeats equity'.

HL **_National Westminster Bank v Morgan_ [1985] AC 686**

Morgan had business difficulties and could not pay the mortgage on the home he jointly owned with his wife. His bank agreed to a new loan to avoid repossession of the family home. In return it gained an unlimited mortgage against the house as security against all of his debts to them. The bank manager met Mrs Morgan and obtained her signature. He assured her in good faith, but incorrectly, that the agreement covered only refinancing of the mortgage on the home when she stated that she lacked confidence in her husband's business and financial abilities. She had no independent advice when signing. The mortgage went into arrears and the bank tried to enforce the surety and claim repossession. The wife counterclaimed, arguing that the signature was obtained by undue influence.

In the Court of Appeal Lord Denning held that the doctrine could be applied wherever there was inequality of bargaining strength. The House of Lords rejected this broad approach. Lord Scarman explained that the relationship was not one that could give rise to a presumption of undue influence and it was insufficient merely to show the relationship. There would also have to be proof that the party alleging undue influence suffered a 'manifest disadvantage' and this was not the case here. The Morgans gained the advantage of being able to stay in their home so there was no duty on the bank to ensure that Mrs Morgan received independent advice

Bank of Credit and Commerce International SA v Aboody
[1990] 1 QB 923

A wife was persuaded by her husband to give a surety on jointly owned property to the bank from which he was taking a business loan. He defaulted on the loan and his wife challenged the bank's action for repossession, arguing undue influence.

The court held that there was undue influence and fixed the bank with constructive or actual notice of the husband's actions in either exercising undue influence over the wife or misrepresenting the amount of money he owed the bank. The transaction was held not to be to her 'manifest disadvantage'. The loan had given the business a good chance of surviving and if it had the transaction would have been to her advantage.

The court redefined the two classes of undue influence:

- Class 1 – actual: where the parties have no special relationship so the party alleging undue influence must prove it.
- Class 2 – presumed: where there is a special relationship so that undue influence is presumed unless disproved.

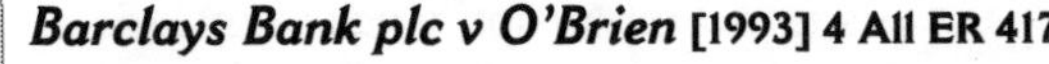

HL **_Barclays Bank plc v O'Brien_ [1993] 4 All ER 417**

The bank granted O'Brien an overdraft for his failing business on the security of a mortgage on his jointly owned marital home. Its representative did not follow the manager's orders to ensure that he and his wife were informed of the nature of the document they were signing and that they should seek independent advice first. They both signed without reading the document. The business collapsed and the bank sought to enforce the surety to recover the debt. Mrs O'Brien countered that her husband had led her to believe that the loan was much smaller and was only for three years.

The Court of Appeal accepted that Mrs O'Brien was induced to sign as a result of her husband's undue influence and had an inaccurate picture of what she had signed. Scott LJ held that:

- she succeeded because, as a wife, she was part of a specially protected class under equity acting as surety for a debt;
- there was a presumption of undue influence against O'Brien;
- this could also apply to cohabitees;
- such sureties were unenforceable when gained by presumed undue influence of the principal debtor;

- the bank could not enforce the surety because it failed to take adequate steps to ensure Mrs O'Brien had a full understanding of what she was committing herself to;
- as a result she could only be liable for the sum that she believed was the actual charge she had agreed to.

The House of Lords differed. Lord Browne-Wilkinson rejected the special equity theory because it would make lending institutions reluctant to make loans on the security of domestic residences. He also felt that the Court of Appeal was extending the scope of presumed undue influence to include wives contrary to precedent. Instead he held that the doctrine of notice should be applied.

- The creditor is put on notice of possible undue influence where *prima facie* the transaction is disadvantageous to the wife, and there is a risk that the husband may have committed a legal or equitable wrong in getting his wife to sign;
- unless the creditor takes reasonable steps to ensure that the surety is entered into with free will and full knowledge then the creditor is fixed with constructive notice of the undue influence;
- constructive notice can be avoided by warning of the risks involved and advising of the need to take independent legal advice at a meeting not attended by the principal debtor.

HL ***Royal Bank of Scotland plc v Etridge (No 2) and other appeals*** **[2001] UKHL 44**

A bank had taken a charge over a wife's property for a loan for her husband's business overdraft. She signed it in the presence of her husband after advice from a solicitor appointed by the bank but whom she later argued was working for her husband. When the bank sought to enforce the charge the wife claimed undue influence by her husband and argued that the solicitor had not explained the charge to her on her own and that the bank was therefore fixed with constructive notice of her husband's undue influence.

The House of Lords reviewed all undue influence cases where wives had stood surety for their husband's debts and applied the basic test in *O'Brien,* i.e. to ask the two basic questions:

- Was the wife subject to her husband's undue influence in signing to agree to the charge?
- Was the bank put on enquiry of the potential undue influence and did they act successfully in avoiding being caught by it?

The House seems to have decided that there are not two types of undue influence and that presumed is evidence to prove undue influence. It also preferred the words 'transactions which are not to be accounted for on terms of charity, love or affection' to 'manifestly disadvantageous' and held that it was out of touch with modern life to presume that each gift from a child to a parent is secured by undue influence. It issued a number of general guidelines:

- Banks should be put on enquiry whenever wives stand surety for their husband's debts and *vice versa.*
- Banks should take reasonable steps to see that wives have been fully informed of the practical implications of the proposed transaction. This need not involve a personal meeting if a suitable alternative is available and if the bank can rely on confirmation from a solicitor acting for the wife that he has advised the her appropriately. However, if the bank was aware that the

solicitor had not properly advised the wife or ought to have realised that the wife had not received appropriate advice it is at risk of being fixed with notice of any undue influence by the husband in securing the wife's agreement to the transaction.

- It is possible for a solicitor advising the wife to act for her husband also (and/or the bank) unless the solicitor realised that there was a real risk of a conflict of interests.
- The advice given by a solicitor should include: the nature of the documents and their practical consequences for the wife; the seriousness of the risks involved i.e. the extent of her financial means and whether she has other assets for repayment; that she has a choice of whether to proceed or not.
- The solicitor should be sure that the wife does wish to proceed, and the discussion should take place at a face-to-face meeting with the wife in the absence of the husband.
- The bank has a duty to obtain confirmation from the solicitor.

For future cases:

- The bank should take steps to check directly with the wife the name of the solicitor he wished to act for her.
- This communication and response must be direct with the wife.
- The bank should give the solicitor the necessary financial information.
- If the bank believes or suspects the wife is being misled by her husband, it should inform the solicitors.

- It should always get written confirmation from the solicitor.

For past transactions it is enough that the bank obtains confirmation from a solicitor acting for the wife that she is informed of the risks.
In obiter the court also stated that the *O'Brien* principle is not confined to husbands and wives but also to others when there is a risk of undue influence (e.g. parent and child). If the bank knows of the relationship this is enough to put it on enquiry.

***Cheese v Thomas* [1994] 1 All ER 35**

The claimant, aged 84, contributed £43,000 to purchase a property costing £83,000 in the sole name of his nephew who provided the other £40,000 on a mortgage. The uncle was to be sole occupant until his death. The nephew defaulted on the mortgage and the claimant sought return of his £43,000, fearful of his security.

The court accepted his claim of undue influence and ordered the house sold. However, the slump in property prices meant that the house could only fetch £55,000 and he was then only entitled to a 43/83 share of the money raised.

***Barclays Bank plc v Boulter and Another* [1997] 2 All ER 1002**

The Boulters bought property on a bank loan, granting a legal charge securing all money owed by them. Mrs Boulter personally covenanted to repay all money. Mr Boulter then borrowed more money and defaulted on the loan. The bank sought possession. Mrs Boulter asked for the charge to be set aside on the basis that she had trusted her husband to manage their finances properly, he had told her the loan was only for the house purchase, and she was not told that the covenant she signed covered all money owed, not just the house. She also argued that the bank might have constructive notice although she did not specifically argue that it did.

The trial judge held that she could not argue constructive notice unless she specifically pleaded it. The Court of Appeal reversed this and held that it was for the bank to disprove its constructive notice. While the House of Lords dismissed the bank's appeal on other grounds, it also held that the Court of Appeal was in error. It was for Mrs Boulter to show that she was a wife living with her husband and that the transaction was manifestly disadvantageous to her, putting the bank on notice of her husband's possible undue influence. The bank would then need to show that it took the appropriate steps to ensure her consent was properly obtained to enforce the charge.

5.4 Illegality

5.4.1 Contracts illegal by statute

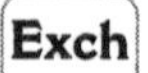

Cope v Rowlands **(1836) 2 M & W 149**

Statute made it illegal for stockbrokers to conduct certain business in London without obtaining a licence. Cope did so and when he sued Rowlands for payment for work done his action failed.

The court held that the lack of a licence made the contract illegal and unenforceable. The provision was to protect the public from the harm that could be caused by unregulated brokers.

5.4.2 Contracts void at common law

HL ***Herbert Morris Ltd v Saxelby*** **[1916] 1 AC 688 HL**

A restraint clause in an employee's contract prevented him after terminating his employment from work in the sale or manufacture of pulley blocks, overhead runways, or overhead travelling cranes for a period of seven years after leaving. His employer's action failed.

The court held that the restraint covered the whole range of the employer's business and the employee's potential expertise and was too wide to succeed despite the key position he had held and the experience he had gained from the employment. It would have deprived him of any employment opportunities.

CA ***Hanover Insurance Brokers Ltd and Christchurch Insurance Brokers Ltd v Schapiro*** **[1994] IRLR 82**

Christchurch bought brokerages including HIB. Three directors of HIB then left and formed their own brokerage and were accused of soliciting clients contrary to a restraint clause in their contracts preventing them from soliciting clients of Hanover Associates, of which HIB was a subsidiary. They argued that the clause was too wide and should be void as they had only worked for HIB.

The court agreed, but held that, since the purpose of the restraint was to prevent soliciting of insurance clients, and only HIB engaged in this activity, the clause could be upheld against them.

***Fitch v Dewes* [1921] 2 AC 158**

An employer sought to enforce a restraint in a solicitor's clerk's contract preventing him from taking similar employment within a seven mile radius of Tamworth town hall.

The court held that the restraint was reasonable. Tamworth was then a small rural community with restricted work for an individual solicitor's practice. The clerk knew the client contact and could have been in a position to damage his employer's business.

***Home Counties Dairies Ltd v Skilton* [1970] 1 WLR 526**

A milkman's contract contained two restraints. Clause 12 prevented him from taking any employment connected with the dairy business. Clause 15 provided that he should not work as a milkman or serve any existing customer one year after leaving the employment.

Clause 12 was held too wide to be reasonable. Potential areas of employment within the dairy industry were vast and the clause would have prevented him from taking a wide range of employment well beyond what he had done and with no chance of damaging his employer's interests. Clause 15 was enforced as it only protected legitimate interests for a short period.

Ch ***Eastham v Newcastle United FC Ltd*** **[1964] Ch 413**

A well-known footballer challenged the legitimacy of the Football Association transfer system. The FA rules meant that a club could retain a player's registration even after his contract had ended and so could be used to prevent him from playing again. Players could be also placed on the transfer list against their will.

The court held that the rules were an unlawful restraint of trade and were unenforceable.

Subsequently the area has become subject to control under Article 39 EC Treaty following the Bosman ruling.

Nordenfelt v Maxim Nordenfelt Co. **[1894] AC 535**

A vendor sold an arms business subject to a restraint preventing the buyer from engaging in the armaments business anywhere in the world for a period of 25 years.

The court enforced the clause as the world was the appropriate market. It was not too wide.

Panayiotou v Sony Music International (UK) Ltd.
[1994] 1 All ER 755

George Michael wanted improved control of his recording contract and release from restrictions it imposed. When part of 'Wham' he had had tried to get their recording contract declared void for restraint of trade. This was changed under an agreed compromise in 1984 and the group moved to CBS. He then became established as a solo artist and in 1988 his contract was changed to reflect this. CBS was also taken over by Sony. He then wished to change his image and became dissatisfied with Sony and sought to have this agreement declared void for restraint of trade.

As the 1988 contract was based on and was an improvement on the 1984 agreement accepted by the court as a genuine compromise it refused his claim as contrary to public policy.

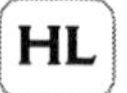

Esso Petroleum Co. Ltd v Harper's Garage (Stourport) Ltd
[1968] AC 269 HL

In a *solus* agreement Esso lent Harper money and Harper could sell only Esso petrol from its two garages. The first agreement was to last for 21 years and Harper was to pay back the loan over that period and not sooner, so was tied to sell only Esso petrol for that period. The second agreement was for four years five months and, unlike the other agreement, had no mortgage to Esso of the land on which the garage was sited. Harper wished to change the brand of petrol it sold and Esso sought an injunction to prevent it.

The court discussed at length and restated the various rules for determining the validity of restraint of trade clauses. Applying these rules it declared that the first agreement was void on the basis of the excessive duration of the restraint. The second agreement was valid, as it was both fair and reasonable.

Lord Reid said: 'Where two experienced traders [bargain] on equal terms and one [agrees the] restraint for reasons which seem good to him the court is in grave danger of stultifying itself if it says that he knows the trader's interests better than he does himself. But there may … be cases where, although the party … restrained has deliberately accepted the main terms … he has been at a disadvantage as regards other terms … then the court may … hold them unreasonable'.

5.4.3 Contracts illegal at common law

CA ***Napier v The National Business Agency*** **[1951] 2 All ER 264**

By his contract of employment, as well as his salary which was set very low, the claimant received expenses of £6 per week where his actual costs were only £1. This had the sole purpose of avoiding income tax since expenses are not subject to taxation. When he was dismissed Napier was owed several weeks' back pay and sued.

The court held that the whole contract was tainted with illegality and unenforceable. Because of the tax avoidance, the agreement was void and the claimant could not recover the money owed to him.

 ***Parkinson v The College of Ambulance*** **[1925] 2 KB 1**

The claimant, who was wealthy, was asked to donate funds to a company in return for which the other party falsely represented that Parkinson would gain a knighthood. He made a donation but when he was not given any honour he sued for return of his money.

It was held to be against public policy to try to secure recognition in this way and the contract was void and unenforceable.

 ***Pearce v Brooks*** **(1866) LR 1 Ex 213**

A prostitute hired carriages for her trade, doing so with the full knowledge of the carriage owner. She failed to pay the fee owed and the owner's action for the price failed.

The contract was for immoral purposes and known to be so by both parties. It was against public policy and unenforceable.

5.4.4 Consequences of contract being declared void

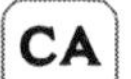 ***Attwood v Lamont*** **[1920] 3 KB 571**

A tailor's cutter was restrained, on leaving employment, from taking up any work as 'tailor, dressmaker, general draper, milliner, hatter, haberdasher, gentleman's, ladies' or children's outfitter at any place within a ten mile radius' of his employer's business.

The court was asked to apply the clause only to the work of tailor's cutter since that was the employee's role, rather than to declare the clause void. The court felt it could not reduce or change the list. It amounted to a comprehensive description of the employer's whole business so severance was not possible; the restraint was too wide and was void and unenforceable.

***Goldsoll v Goldman* [1915] 1 Ch 292**

A restraint in a contract for sale of a jewellery business prevented the vendor from selling real or imitation jewellery in the UK, Isle of Man, France, USA, Russia, Spain etc. The buyer tried to enforce it.

The business only specialised in sale of imitation jewellery and had no export market. The court severed the word 'real' because it was unnecessary to the protection of the business, and limited it to the UK. The rest of the clause was upheld.

Lord Cozens-Hardy commented: 'It is admitted that the business of a dealer in real jewellery is not the same as that of a dealer in imitation jewellery … so it is difficult to support the whole of this provision, for [it] must be limited to what is reasonably necessary for the protection of the covenantee's business'.

5.4.5 Consequences of contract being declared illegal

 ***Tinsley v Milligan* [1993] 3 WLR 126**

The two parties jointly bought a house in the first party's name so that the second party could make fraudulent claims for state benefits. The second party later tried to claim a share of the property under a resulting trust arising out of her contribution to the purchase of the house. The first party argued that the agreement was void for illegality and unenforceable.

The court held that the second party was not merely trying to enforce an illegal contract but was asserting a property right arising under a trust so the agreement was enforceable. The House rejected the argument that the contract should be void because it was against public conscience but preferred to find that the potential illegality of the agreement had no bearing on the case in hand. Lord Goff dissented, and felt that to enforce a trust required the party seeking this to come to court with clean hands, which she had not.

 ***Hall v Woolston Hall Leisure Ltd* [2000] 4 All ER 787**

The claimant was dismissed when she became pregnant and alleged sex discrimination contrary to the Employment Rights Act 1996. The employer claimed that the contract of employment was itself illegal and unenforceable because the claimant was aware that the employer was paying and recording her wages in such a way as to defraud the Inland Revenue of tax.

The court held that the illegality was caused by the employer and was irrelevant to the claim, so compensation for unfair dismissal was possible. While the claimant was aware of the arrangement it was for the employer's benefit and she had no control over it.

CHAPTER 6

DISCHARGE OF A CONTRACT

Discharge by performance:
The basic rule is that in an entire contract all obligations must be preformed *Cutter v Powell*
An exception is where part performance is freely accepted *Sumpter v Hedges*
Or where a party has substantially performed *Hoenig v Isaacs*
A party is not bound to perform when he has been prevented by the other party *Planche v Colburn*

Discharge by agreement:
Parties can agree to end obligations by each providing consideration for a fresh agreement to end existing obligations *British Russian Gazette Ltd v Associated Newspapers Ltd*

Discharge

Discharge by frustration:
Traditionally parties were bound by absolute obligations to perform *Paradine v Jane*
This was unfair so a principle developed ending the obligation to perform where an unforeseen event beyond the control of either party made it impossible to perform *Taylor v Caldwell*
This might include subsequent illegality *Denny, Mott & Dickson Ltd v James B Fraser & Co. Ltd*
And commercial sterilisation of the contract *Krell v Henry*
But self-induced frustration will not relieve a party of obligations *Maritime National Fish Ltd v Ocean Trawlers Ltd*
Nor will it where the contract is merely more onerous to perform *Davis Contractors Ltd v Fareham UDC*
It is possible now to recover for money spent out in advance of a frustrated contract *Fibrosa Spolka Akcyjna v Fairbairn Lawson Combe Barbour Ltd* (The Fibrosa case)
And the Law Reform (Frustrated Contracts) Act 1943 s 1(3) allows recovery to prevent unjust enrichment *BP Exploration Co. (Libya) Ltd v Hunt (No. 2)*

Discharge by breach:
Whether the victim of a breach can repudiate or sue for damages depends on the nature of the term breached *Bunge Corporation v Tradax Export SA*
In an anticipatory breach a party can sue immediately or wait for the breach *Hochster v De la Tour*
This may cause the party to lose his remedy if an unforeseen event then frustrates the contract *Avery v Bowden*

6.1 Discharge by performance

6.1.1 The strict rule of performance

CP ***Cutter v Powell***
(1795) 6 Term Rep 320

Cutter enlisted as second mate for the whole voyage on a ship but died before it was complete. His widow sued on a '*quantum meruit*' basis (for the amount of work done) but failed in her action.

The court held that it was an 'entire' contract requiring absolute performance. Since Cutter died during the voyage he had failed to complete his contract and the ship owner was not obliged to pay. By committing himself to the whole voyage Cutter stood to earn nearly four times what he would have done on the normal rate.

Ashhurst J said 'as [the contract] is entire, and … depends on a condition precedent … the condition must be performed before [he] is entitled to receive any thing under it'.

6.1.2 Ways of avoiding the strict rule

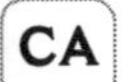

CA ***Sumpter v Hedges*** **[1898] 1 QB 673**

A builder was contracted to build two houses and stables. He had completed some of the work when he ran out of money and was unable to complete it. The landowner then had the work completed using the materials left by the builder who sued for his fee.

The court held that the builder could receive the cost of the materials used but rejected his argument that part performance had been accepted by the landowner. The landowner had no choice but find an alternative way of completing the work or leave the buildings partly completed. He had not freely accepted part performance.

Hoenig v Isaacs **[1952] 2 All ER 176**

A decorator contracted to decorate and furnish a flat for £750. The owner moved into the flat and paid £400 in three instalments while the work was being done. Because of defects costing about £55 to repair, he refused to pay the balance. The decorator sued.

The court held that the contract was substantially performed and only differing from the contract in minor respects. It ordered that the balance should be paid less a sum representing the defects.

Bolton v Mahadeva [1972] 1 WLR 1009, where the cost of repair was too great a proportion of the original cost of installation for the court to accept that the work had been substantially performed.

Planche v Colburn **(1831) 8 Bing 14**

A publisher hired the claimant, to write a book in a series he was planning to produce. The publisher then abandoned the series and the author was prevented from finishing the book though he had already done much work. His claim for *quantum meruit* succeeded.

The court awarded the author half his fee as he was prevented from performing. He could also have claimed for anticipatory breach.

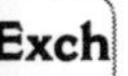

Startup v Macdonald **(1843) 6 Man & G 593**

In a contract for 10 tons of linseed oil to be delivered by the end of March the supplier delivered at 8.30 pm on Saturday March 31st and the buyer refused to accept delivery.

The court held that the supplier had tendered performance and could recover damages as a result.

The answer might be different now under the Sale of Goods Act 1979 since delivery should be at a 'reasonable hour'.

6.2 Discharge by agreement

British Russian Gazette Ltd v Associated Newspapers Ltd **[1933] 2 KB 616**

The claimant offered to forgo libel actions against a newspaper in return for £1,050 in full satisfaction of any settlement and costs he might receive. Before payment was made he brought the actions.

The court rejected his argument that there could be no accord and satisfaction until payment was made. The offer to forgo the actions and the response were good consideration by which he was bound.

6.3 Discharge by frustration

6.3.1 The purpose and development of the doctrine

***Paradine v Jane* (1647) Aleyn 26**

Paradine claimed rent due under a lease. Jane's defence was that he was ejected by an army for three years of the lease.

The court held that there was an absolute obligation to pay the rent, which was unaffected by the intervening event. If he had wished to reduce his liability for intervening events preventing performance then he should have made express provision for it in the lease.

QB ***Taylor v Caldwell***
(1863) 32 LJ QB 164

Taylor agreed to rent a music hall from Caldwell for concerts and fetes. After the contract date but before the concerts were due the music hall burnt down and performance was impossible. There were no contractual stipulations for what should happen in the event of fire. Taylor had spent money on advertising and other preparations and sued Caldwell for damages but failed.

The court held that the commercial purpose of the contract had ceased to exist, performance was impossible, and so both sides were excused from further performance of their obligations.

Blackburn J stated: 'in contracts in which performance depends on the continued existence of a given person or thing, a condition is implied that the impossibility of performance arising from the perishing of the person or thing shall excuse the performance'.

6.3.2 The different types of frustrating events

KB ***Morgan v Manser*** **[1948] 1 KB 184**

A music hall artiste was contracted to his manager for 10 years from 1938. Between 1940 and 1946 he was conscripted into the armed forces during the war so could not complete his duties.

The court held that his absence undermined the central purpose of the contract and so both parties were excused performance.

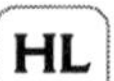

Denny, Mott & Dickson Ltd v James B Fraser & Co. Ltd [1944] 1 All ER 678

In July 1914 a contract was formed for construction of a reservoir and water works within a six-year period. In 1916 a government order stopped the work and requisitioned most of the plant.

The court held that the contract was frustrated at the time of the government order. It was impossible for the parties to continue performance past that point because of subsequent illegality.

Krell v Henry [1903] 2 KB 740

The defendant rented a room overlooking the procession route for the coronation of King Edward VII for two days in 1902 with no specific mention of the purpose of the hire in the written agreement. When the coronation was postponed because of the king's illness the defendant refused to pay for the room.

The court accepted that the contract was frustrated. Watching the procession was the 'foundation of the contract, further performance was relieved and he was not bound to pay for the room'.

Chandler v Webster [1904] 1 KB 493 (p 119).

Herne Bay Steamboat Co. v Hutton **[1903] 2 KB 683**

Part of the coronation celebrations was to be a review of the fleet by the newly crowned king. The defendant hired a boat to watch the review and to sail round the Solent to see the fleet which was rarely together in port. His claim that the contract was frustrated failed.

The court held that there was no frustration. One purpose had been thwarted but it was still possible to use the boat and to see the fleet. The commercial value of the contract had not disappeared completely.

Vaughan Williams LJ said: 'I see nothing to differentiate this contract from [where a] person engaged a cab to take him on … three days to Epsom to see the race, and [through e.g.] spread of an infectious disease or an anticipation of a riot, the races are prohibited. In such a case … he would [not] be relieved of his bargain'.

6.3.3 The limitations on the doctrine of frustration

Maritime National Fish Ltd v Ocean Trawlers Ltd **[1935] AC 524**

Maritime owned four trawlers but wished to use five so chartered another. Each needed a licence from the Canadian Government before it could be used. Maritime applied for five licences but was only granted three. It had to name the trawlers to which the licences applied and used three of its own, claimed that the charter had been frustrated, and refused to pay for the hire of the trawler.

The court rejected the claim that the contract was frustrated. Maritime could have used one of the licences for the chartered vessel but chose to apply them to its own. It was not prevented from completing its obligations by an intervening event, any frustration was self-induced and it was bound to pay for the hire of the vessel.

HL ***Davis Contractors Ltd v Fareham UDC*** **[1956] AC 696**

Builders tried to claim frustration to avoid a contract when shortages of building supplies meant that they would take much longer to complete the work than they had envisaged and would lose profit.

The court would not accept that mere hardship or inconvenience was a ground justifying a claim of frustration.

CA ***Amalgamated Investment & Property Co. Ltd v John Walker & Sons Ltd*** **[1977] 1 WLR 164**

Walker contracted to sell a building, identified in the contract as suitable for development, to the Investment Company who wanted it for that purpose. It made no enquiries on whether the building was of historic or architectural interest and the defendants were not aware at the time of the contract that it was. Unknown to either party the Department of the

Environment then listed the building, meaning that it was of historical or architectural interest as a result of which it could not be used for property development. The value dropped by £1.5 million from the contract price of £1.71 million.

The court rejected the argument that the contract was frustrated because of the listing and held that this was a common risk associated with old buildings. The developers, as specialists in the property market, should have known this. An argument that the contract was void for common mistake also failed, since the mistake was not operative when the contract was made.

Ch ***Jackson v Union Marine Insurance Ltd*** **(1874) LR 10 CP 125**

A ship was chartered for a cargo voyage but ran aground and could not be loaded for some time. Frustration was claimed.

The court held that a term should be implied into the contract that the ship should be available for loading in a reasonable time. The long delay in loading frustrated the contract as it was impossible to perform the contract within a reasonable time.

6.3.4 The common law effects of frustration

Chandler v Webster **[1904] 1 KB 493**

In similar facts to *Krell v Henry* (1903) a party hired a room in a position along the route of the coronation procession to watch it. However, unlike *Krell v Henry*, where the room was to be paid for on the day, here the room was paid for in advance.

The court accepted that the contract was frustrated but would not allow recovery of the money already paid as obligations cease at the point of frustration.

This is unsatisfactory and possibly unfair because the outcome depends entirely on the point reached in the contract when the frustrating event occurs so inconsistent results are possible.

Fibrosa Spolka Akcyjna v Fairbairn Lawson Combe Barbour Ltd (The Fibrosa case) **[1943] AC 32**

In a contract for sale of machinery to a Polish company, before it could be performed delivery was made impossible because Germany invaded Poland before the start of the Second World War. The contract contained a 'war clause' and it was argued that there was no frustration as the clause covered the event in question.

The House of Lords held that the contract was still frustrated because the clause only provided for delays in delivery, not for the more dramatic consequences of invasion.

6.3.5 The Law Reform (Frustrated Contracts) Act 1943

BP Exploration Co. (Libya) Ltd v Hunt (No.2)
[1979] 1 WLR 783

BP granted Hunt a concession to explore for oil in Libya and to drill for any found. BP agreed financed the project for a half share of the concession and set expenses at three eighths of the oil found until it recovered 125% of its outlay. Hunt discovered a large oil field and began drilling but the Libyan Government then claimed all rights to it frustrating the contract. BP had actually recovered only a small amount of its expenses and sued successfully under s 1(3) of the Law Reform (Frustrated Contracts) Act 1943 since Hunt had gained a valuable benefit from the oil already drilled, and compensation from the Libyan Government.

At first instance Goff J stated that any sum awarded should be based not on what BP had spent to finance the arrangement but on the benefit already enjoyed by Hunt in order to prevent his 'unjust enrichment' at their expense. He approached s 1(3)(b) on the basis that it involves two tasks: first, the identification of the 'valuable benefit', and secondly, the determination of the 'just sum' to be awarded, the amount of which is capped by the 'valuable benefit'. He came to the conclusion that 'benefit' means the 'end product' of what the claimant has provided, not the value of the work that has been done. The Court of Appeal and House of Lords both upheld the decision but without further comment on s 1(3).

Section 1(3) of the Law Reform (Frustrated Contracts) Act 1943 obviously helps to prevent some of the unfairness in the previous law but has limitations. It can only be used if a party has gained a valuable benefit before the frustrating event. If none is gained by the other party before then and no money is payable then either it cannot be used to recover for work already completed.

6.4 Discharge by breach

6.4.1 The different types of breach

Bunge Corporation v Tradax Export SA **[1981] 1 WLR 711**

The buyer was required by a contract to give at least 15 days' notice of readiness to load a vessel, and gave only 13.

The court held that there was a breach justifying repudiation. Lord Wilberforce explained that as the sellers' obligation to ship was a condition the obligation to give notice to load in proper time should be also. The consequences of the breach were irrelevant. They were in fact minor, which was why the first instance judge had felt repudiation inappropriate but Lord Wilberforce felt that stipulations as to time in mercantile contracts should be viewed as conditions.

Hochster v De la Tour **[1853] 2 E & B 678**

The claimant was hired to begin work as a courier two months after the contract date. One month later the defendants wrote to him and cancelled the contract. He immediately sued successfully.

The court rejected the argument that the claimant could not sue till the due date. There was no requirement that the victim of a breach of contract must wait until the contract is in fact breached before suing. It was sufficient that he knew that a breach would occur.

Lord Campbell CJ explained 'it is … more rational, and …for the benefit of both parties, that, after … renunciation of the agreement … the plaintiff should be at liberty to consider himself absolved from any further performance … retaining his right to sue for any damage … instead of remaining idle and laying out money in preparations which must be useless, he is at liberty to seek service under another employer, which would go to mitigation of the damages'.

6.4.2 The consequences of breach

Avery v Bowden **(1855) 5 E & B 714**

Bowden contracted to load cargo on a ship for Avery. Before the due date it became clear that Bowden could not perform. Avery could have sued at this point but waited hoping that the contract would be completed, but intending to sue if it was not. The contract was then frustrated by the outbreak of the Crimean War.

The court held that obligations ceased at the point of frustration and Avery was left without a remedy for the breach.

This obviously leaves the victim of an anticipatory breach with a difficult decision whether to sue or to wait.

White and Carter Ltd v McGregor **[1962] AC 413**

A party was to supply litter bins for a local council. The bins were to be paid for from revenue from businesses placing advertisements on the bins for three years. One business backed out before the bins were complete. The bin supplier still prepared the advertising, using it for the whole contract period, then sued for the full price.

The court accepted that the victim of an anticipatory breach is not bound to end his own obligations merely because of the other party's breach.

CHAPTER 7

REMEDIES

Damages:
The breach must be the factual cause of the damage *London Joint Stock Bank v MacMillan*
And must be a loss naturally arising from the breach or one in the contemplation of both parties when the contract was formed *Hadley v Baxendale*
A claimant can recover for loss of a valuable amenity *Farley v Skinner*
And even for an account of profits illegally gained *Attorney-General v Blake*
But the claimant has a duty to mitigate the loss *British Westinghouse Electric and Manufacturing Co. Ltd v Underground Electric Railways Co. of London Ltd*
Claimants can also recover for a 'mental distress' although this is generally limited to where the contract is one for pleasure *Jackson v Horizon Holidays*
For liquidated damages the sum must fairly represent an accurate assessment of the likely loss and not be a mere penalty *Dunlop Pneumatic Tyre Co v New Garage and Motor Co*

Remedies

Quantum meruit:
Possible to gain a sum representing the work already done under a contract *Upton RDC v Powell*

Equitable remedies:
Specific performance:
The remedy enforces completion of a contract so is only granted where it is possible for the court to oversee it *Ryan v Mutual Tontine Westminster Chambers Association*
Injunctions:
Can be used to protect legitimate interests so this will not include where the injunction has the effect of preventing the other party from working *Page One Records v Britton*
Rescission:
This remedy puts the parties back to their pre-contractual position so that must in fact be possible *Clarke v Dickson*
And delay defeats equity *Long v Lloyd*
Rectification:
A contractual document may be changed where it does not accurately reflect the actual agreement *Craddock Bros Ltd v Hunt*

7.1 Unliquidated damages

7.1.1 Tests of causation and remoteness of damage

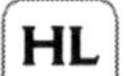
HL

London Joint Stock Bank v MacMillan **[1918] AC 777**

Clients of banks are contractually bound to write their cheques so that they cannot be easily altered. Here the client failed in this duty and a third party altered the cheque, causing the bank loss.

The court held the client liable for the loss because he had directly caused it by failing in his duty.

Exch ***Hadley v Baxendale*** **(1854) 9 Exch 341**

A mill owner contracted with a carrier for delivery of a crankshaft to his mill. The mill was out of action because the existing crankshaft was broken. The carrier did not know when the contract was formed that the mill owner had no spare crankshaft. Delivery was very late and in that time the claimant was unable to grind corn and supply his customers. He sued unsuccessfully for his lost profit.

The court held that there was no liability since the loss was not one in the defendant's contemplation when the contract was formed.

Alderson B said: 'damages ... should be such as may ... reasonably be considered arising either naturally, i.e. according to the usual course of things ... or such as may be reasonably supposed to have been in the contemplation of both parties at the time they made the contract as the probable result of the breach'.

Victoria Laundry Ltd v Newman Industries Ltd
[1949] 2 KB 528

The defendant contracted to deliver a boiler to the claimant but failed to do so for five months. The claimant sued for loss of its usual profits of £16 per week from the date of the breach and also for lost profits of £262 per week from a government contract that it had been unable to fulfil without the new boiler.

The court accepted the claim for the usual profits as this was a natural consequence loss and the claimant had made it clear to the defendant that it urgently needed the boiler fitted by the due date. It rejected the latter action as the government contract was unknown to the defendant when the contract was formed. Asquith LJ said the two heads of *Hadley v Baxendale* represent a single principle of remoteness based on different tests of foreseeability and said:

- to indemnity a claimant for any loss no matter how remote is too harsh a test to apply to the defendant;
- recoverable loss should be measured against what is reasonably foreseeable to result from the breach;

- foreseeability of loss depends on the knowledge possessed at the time of formation, which could be:
  - common knowledge – what any reasonable person would be expected to know would arise from the breach,
  - actual knowledge of the parties at the time of formation;
- knowledge can be implied on the basis of what a reasonable man MAY have contemplated in the circumstances rather than what a reasonable man MUST have contemplated.

***H Parsons (Livestock) Ltd v Uttley Ingham* [1978] QB 791**

In a contract for sale and installation of an animal feed hopper with a ventilated cover, the cover was sealed for transit but the installers then forgot to open it. As a result the feed became mouldy and the claimant's pigs died. The claimant sued successfully.

The first instance judge held the loss was too remote and not within the contemplation of the defendant. This was reversed by the Court of Appeal. Lord Denning distinguished between loss of profit, where a test of remoteness based on contract should apply, and property damage, as here, where he felt the test should be the same test of foreseeability as in tort. In the House of Lords Lord Scarman rejected this distinction and held that the loss was only an example of what should be in the contemplation of the parties on formation.

7.1.2 The bases of assessment

***Farley v Skinner* [2001] 3 WLR 899 HL**

The claimant hired a surveyor before buying a house, to

prepare a report on whether the property was affected by aircraft noise. The report stated that it was not but this was wrong and also negligent as the house was near a beacon for stacking aircraft at busy times. The claimant paid £490,000 for the house and spent £125,000 on it before moving in. When he discovered the noise he decided not to move but sued the surveyor for damages for loss of amenity.

The House of Lords held that for loss of amenity to succeed, it was not essential that the contract was to provide pleasure, relaxation etc. The claimant did not forfeit his right to non-pecuniary damages by not moving and he was awarded £10,000.

Ruxley Electronics and Construction Ltd v Forsyth; Laddingford Enclosures Ltd v Forsyth [1995] 3 All ER 268 (p 131).

HL ***Attorney-General v Blake* [2001] 1 AC 268**

A British Secret Service agent had passed secrets to the Russians during the Cold War and was convicted but escaped to Russia where he remained. He later wrote an autobiography and received advances on his fee. The book included details of his work in the secret service. This was illegal as he was still bound by the Official Secrets Act 1989 and was a breach of contract. The Attorney-General sought to prevent him from claiming the money still owed.

The Court of Appeal allowed an injunction against Blake and on damages held that, without the Attorney-General showing loss by the government, these were only nominal. To avoid

Blake profiting from his crimes and breach of contract it held that restitution could be used as it was an exceptional case. Blake failed to provide the full service he contracted to give and had obtained a profit, the payment for the book, for doing the thing he had contracted not to do, breaching his promise of secrecy. The House of Lords upheld the Court of Appeal reasoning and allowed the Attorney-General a full account of Blake's profits. There was no reason in principle why such an award could not be made in exceptional circumstances such as existed here, but it was vague on when these might arise.

7.1.3 The duty to mitigate

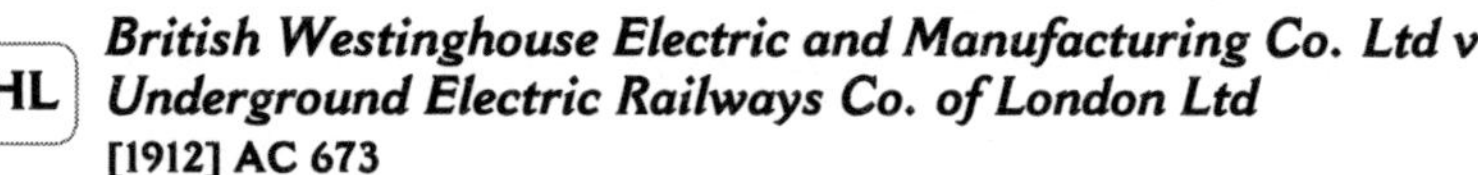

HL ***British Westinghouse Electric and Manufacturing Co. Ltd v Underground Electric Railways Co. of London Ltd***
[1912] AC 673

British Westinghouse contracted to supply turbines to Underground Electric Railways. When the goods were delivered they did not match the contract specifications and as a result the buyers had to replace them with turbines bought from another supplier. These were so efficient that they soon paid for the difference between the contract price and the actual value of the goods in the first contract.

The court held that only those losses sustained before the original turbines were replaced were recoverable.

Lord Haldane LC said: a claimant must take all 'reasonable steps to mitigate the loss consequent on the breach [which] debars him from claiming in respect of … damage which is due to his neglect'.

7.1.4 The 'mental distress' cases

***Jackson v Horizon Holidays* [1975] 1 WLR 1468**

In a contract for a holiday the hotel was dirty, promised facilities were absent and the food was poor, contrary to the description.

The claimant was given damages not only for his own mental distress but for that suffered by his family also. The court held that the distress suffered by the family was a loss to the overall contract so the claimant received much less than he bargained for. The claim succeeded because in holiday contracts the provision of comfort, pleasure and peace of mind is a central purpose.

Jarvis v Swan Tours Ltd [1973] 1 QB 23 and *Woodar Investment Development Ltd v Wimpey Construction UK Ltd* [1980] 1 All ER 571 which limited the scope for mental distress.

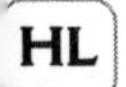

***Ruxley Electronics and Construction Ltd v Forsyth; Laddingford Enclosures Ltd v Forsyth* [1995] 3 All ER 268 HL**

In a contract to construct a swimming pool the purchaser stipulated a maximum depth of 7' 6". The pool when completed was only 6' 9" and the diving area was only 6'. This prevented the purchaser from safely enjoying the pleasure of diving into the pool.

The House of Lords awarded damages for loss of amenity.

7.2 Liquidated damage clauses

Dunlop Pneumatic Tyre Co v New Garage and Motor Co. **[1914] AC 79**

In its contract with Dunlop a garage was bound to pay £5 in respect of breaches such as selling the tyres under the manufacturer's recommended price. When it did so Dunlop sued.

The House of Lords considered that the sum was a genuine assessment of loss and not a penalty. Lord Dunedin developed a test for establishing genuine liquidated damages:

- An extravagant sum is always a penalty.
- Payment of a large sum for not settling a small debt is a penalty.
- A single sum in respect of a variety of breaches is a penalty.
- The wording in the contract is not conclusive.
- Where assessment of the actual loss before the contract is made is impossible this will not prevent recovery.

7.3 Claims for *quantum meruit*

Upton RDC v Powell **[1942] 1 All ER 220**

A retained fireman (a part-time employee only attending when there is a fire or other call-out) had provided services even though there was no fixed agreement as to what wages would be payable.

The court awarded a sum that it considered reasonable.

7.4 Equitable remedies

7.4.1 Specific performance

Ryan v Mutual Tontine Westminster Chambers Association **[1893] 1 Ch 116**

In a tenancy agreement the landlord was obliged to provide a hall porter to maintain the common areas. This employee failed to do the work properly.

A claim for specific performance was refused because it would have been impossible for the court to supervise the work.

Posner v Scott-Lewis [1987] Ch 25 where no porter had been appointed and the order could easily be enforced.

7.4.2 Injunctions

Fellowes v Fisher **[1976] QB 122**

A restraint in a conveyancing clerk's contract prevented him from taking similar employment in Walthamstow for five years.

Lord Denning held that the restraint was unreasonable and unenforceable. The clerk was relatively unknown to clients. The employer was not genuinely protecting a legitimate interest.

Faccenda Chicken v Fowler [1986] 1 All ER 617

Fowler was sales manager of a company selling fresh chickens. He developed a new sales strategy. When he left to set up on his own his employer sought an injunction.

This was denied because the termination was reasonable and there was no express restraint in the contract.

Ch *Page One Records v Britton* [1968] 1 WLR 157

'The Troggs', a well-known sixties pop group, were contractually bound indefinitely to their manager and could not at any time appoint another manager. Other terms were equally unfavourable. They found a new manager and the existing manager tried to enforce the contract through means of an injunction but failed.

The court would not grant an order as it felt that the effect would be to tie the group to their manager indefinitely and against their will or otherwise to prevent them from working as musicians.

7.4.3 Rescission

QB **_Clarke v Dickson_ [1858] 120 ER 463**

Clarke bought partnership shares after misrepresentations made before the contract. Later the partnership became a limited company. When the company was wound up Clarke then discovered the misrepresentation and sought rescission and return of the money he had paid on entry.

The court would not rescind because the nature of the shares had changed from partnership to company. The judge explained how *restitutio in integrum* applies. If a butcher buys live cattle, slaughters them and later discovers a defect in the contract and wishes to rescind, it would be denied. The state of the cattle would have changed so dramatically that it would be impossible to put the parties back into their pre-contract position.

Long v Lloyd [1958] 1 WLR 753

The claimant bought a lorry that proved to be defective contrary to the contract description. Defects were immediately apparent but the purchaser twice allowed the seller to make repairs to the lorry.

The court held he had affirmed the contract so could not rescind.

7.4.4 Rectification of a document

Craddock Bros Ltd v Hunt [1923] 2 Ch 136

Craddock sold his house to Hunt, not intending an adjoining yard to be included in the sale. By mistake it was in the conveyance.

Craddock's action for rectification succeeded as the document did not reflect the actual agreement.

INDEX

acceptance 1, 9–10
  communication 14–16
  counter offers 10–12
  notification 4
  and performance 5
  silence 14
  standard forms 12–13
  and withdrawal 7
actionable misrepresentation 74
actual undue influence 95
advertisements 5
agreement, discharge of contract 113–14
ancillary terms 60–1
anticipatory breach 123–4

bilateral contract 5
breach of contract 110
  anticipatory 123–4
  counter offers 8, 10
  damages 61, 62, 126–8
  discharge of contract 122–4
  effect of terms 49
  fundamental 67–9
  implied terms 56–7, 59–60
  revocation 8, 123
business arrangements 1, 13, 16
  capacity of corporations 35–7
  implied terms 49, 55–6
  legal relations 31–4

capacity 35
  corporations 35–7
  minors 37–40
coercion of will 91
collateral promise 46–7
comfort letter 34
common law
  frustration 119–20
  illegal contracts 105–6
  immoral contracts 73, 106
  terms 49, 56–7
  void contracts 40, 101–5
common mistake 73, 81, 83, 88
communication 1
  electronic methods 15–16
  of offers 6–7
  postal method 14–15
  of revocation 8
Companies Act 1985 37
condition precedent 111
conditions
  advertisement 5
  contract 49
consideration 1
  definitions 17
  existing duties 22–4
  extra benefit 25–6, 28
  past 20–1
  Pinnel's rule 26–7
  privity rule 21–2, 41–2
  promissory estoppel 27–8
  third parties 41, 42
  value of 18–20
constructive notice 96, 100
Consumer Credit Act 1974 57
Consumer Protection (Distance Selling) Regulations 2000 16
contract, nature of *see also* discharge of contract
  bilateral 5
  purchase of product 5
  timing of formation 1, 2–3
  unilateral 8
Contracts (Rights of Third Parties) Act 1999 22

contrary intent 1
corporations
  business arrangements 1, 13, 16
  capacity 35–7
corruption 73
counter offers 1
  acceptance 10–12
  breach of contract 8, 10
creditworthiness 85, 86
custom and usage 54

damages 125 *see also quantum meruit*
  assessment 128–30
  breach of contract 61, 62, 126–8
  causation 126–7
  fraud 77
  fundamental breach 68
  liquidated 132
  mental distress 131–2
  'merchantable' quality 61–2
  Misrepresentation Act 1967 79
  mitigation of loss 130
  remoteness 127–8
debt, and minors 39–40
'delay defeats equity' 93
discharge of contract 110
  by agreement 113–14
  by breach 122–4
  by frustration 114–22
  by performance 111–13
domestic arrangements 1, 28–31
duress 73, 89–90
  economic 90–2
duty of care
deed 44–5
  negligence 77–8

E-Commerce (EU Directive)
    Regulations 2003 16
economic duress 73, 90–2
electronic communications 1, 15–16
Employer's Liability Act 1880 38
employment contracts *see* restraint of
    trade clauses
employment of minors 38–9
Employment Rights Act 1996 108
equitable remedies 125
  injunctions 133–4
  rectification 136
  rescission 135
  specific performance 133
equity 80
  delay 93
  minors 40
  mistake 83–4, 87–8
'Errington' principle 9
estoppel 27
ex gratia payments 31–2
exchange, consideration 17
exclusion clauses 49
  fundamental breach 67–9
  inclusion in contract 63–6
  liability 52
  negligence 63–4, 67
  oral misrepresentation 66
  reasonableness 70–1
  unfair surprise 72
express terms 51–3

face-to-face dealings 73, 87, 98
family relationships 1, 28–31
  undue influence 96–9
foreseeability 127–8
forfeiture agreements 45
formation of contract 1–3
forms, standard 12–13
fraud
  by minors 39–40
  misrepresentation 73, 76–7
fraudulent misrepresentation 73, 76–7
frustration 110
  claims for 118–19
  common law effects 119–20
  performance prevented 114–17
  self-induced 117–18
  valuable benefit 121–2
fundamental breach 67–9

'Hedley Byrne' principle 77–8
Hire Purchase Act 1964 79
honest opinion 50
'honour pledge' clause 33

illegality 73
  consequences of 106–9
  contract illegal 105–7
  contract void 101–5
  by statute 100–1

immoral contracts 73, 106
impersonation 74
implied terms 52, 54–6
  common law 56–7
  Sale of Goods Act 1979 49, 62, 71
  statute law 57–60
injunctions 125, 133–4
innominate terms 49, 62
intention
  commercial arrangements 31–4
  domestic arrangements 28–31
  implied terms 55–6
invitation to tender 6
invitation to treat 1, 2–3
  advertisements 5
  invitation to tender 6

judicial control
  exclusion clauses 63–6
  terms of contract 61–2
jus quaesitum tertio 42

Law of Property Act 1925 47–8
Law Reform (Frustrated Contracts) Act 1943 121–2
legal relations 1
  commercial arrangements 32–4
  ex gratia payment 31–2
  intention to create 29–31
  purely domestic 28
liability
  disclaimer 77
  exclusion clause 52
  limited 45–6, 70
limitation clauses 68–9, 70–1
  third parties 43, 45–6
liquidated damages 132
loss of amenity 129, 131–2

meaning, of words 69
mental distress 125, 131–2
'merchantable' quality 59, 61–2
mere puff 4–5
mere representations 49, 50–1
minors 35, 37–40
Minors' Contracts Act 1987 40
misrepresentation 73
  damages 79
  definitions of 74–5
  duty of care 77–8
  equity 80
  express terms 51–2
  fraud 76–7
  negligence 50–1, 78–9
  non-disclosure 80
  opinion 50–1
  oral 66
  rescission 135
Misrepresentation Act 1967 51, 73, 78, 79
mistake 73
  common 81, 83, 88
  creditworthiness 85, 86
  equity 87–8
  identity of party 85–7
  mutual 84
  non est factum 88–9
  operative 82–4, 86
mitigation of loss 130
modern world, effect on law 13, 16
mutual mistake 73

necessary goods, minors 37–8
negligence
  contributory 79
  exclusion clauses 63–4, 67
  misrepresentation 50–1
  valid disclaimer 77–8
negligent misrepresentation 73
nemo dat quod non habet 87
non-disclosure 80
non est factum 88–9
notice, doctrine of 96
  constructive 100

objects clauses 35–7
'O'Brien' principle 95–9
Offensive Weapons Act 1959 2
offers 1, 4–6
  communication of 6–7
  invitation to treat 2–3
  revocation 7–9
  termination 9
  withdrawal 3–4
Official Secrets Act 1989 129
'officious bystander' test 57
operative mistake 82–4, 86
opinion 50–1

oral
  assurance 53
  misrepresentation 66

'parol evidence' rule 53, 84
part performance 111–12
past consideration 20–1
performance 1, 110
  acceptance 5
  and mistake 88
  prevention of 114–17
  specific 125, 133
  strict rule 111–13
  unilateral contract 8–9
  unilateral offer 5
Pharmacy and Poisons Act 1933 2
Pinnel's rule 26–7
postal communications 1, 14–15
presumed undue influence 95–6, 97
previous dealings 63–4, 67
privity rule 21–2, 41–2
  exceptions 42–8
promissory estoppel 27–8
property, meaning of 48
Protection of Birds Act 1954 3
protest, level of 92
public policy 104, 106

quantum meruit 12, 111, 113, 125, 132–3

real property 48
'reasonableness' test 49, 70–1, 128
  exclusion clauses 70–1
  restraint of trade 102–3, 105
rectification 125, 136
referential bid 6
remoteness of damage 126–8
representations 49, 50–1 *see also* misrepresentation
repudiation of contract 60–1, 62, 122
res extincta 81
res sua 82
rescission 125, 135
restitutio in integrum 135
restitution 40, 130
restraint of trade clauses 73
  illegal 105–7
  unreasonable 133–4
  void contracts 101–5
Restrictive Trade Practices Act 1976 42
resulting trust 108
revocation of offer 4, 7–9
  breach of contract 123

Sale of Goods Act 1893 52
Sale of Goods Act 1979
  implied terms 49, 58–60, 62, 71
  minors 38
  mistake 81
  'reasonable hour' 113
'set aside in equity' 83
silence 1, 14
specific performance 125, 133
standard forms 12–13, 53
statutory law
  exclusion clauses 63–6
  implied terms 49, 57–60
substantial performance 112
sue, rights to 42

telex 15–16
tenders 6
termination of offer 9
terms 49, 60–1
  common law 56–7
  express 51–3
  and facts 54–6
  judicial discretion 61–2
  misrepresentation 51–2
  statute law 57–60
third parties *see also* privity rule
  collateral promise 46–7
  consideration 41, 47
  duty of care 44–5
  forfeiture agreements 45
  limitation clauses 43, 45–6
  property 47–8
  trusts 42–3
timing of contract 2–3
  method of communication 14–16
trusts 42–3, 108

uberrimae fidei 80
ultra vires doctrine 35–7
undue influence 73, 90, 93
  classes of 95, 97

constructive notice 94, 96, 97, 100
professional responsibility 94–9
special equity 95–6
unenforceable contracts
domestic arrangements 28–9
minors 39–40
past consideration 20–1
vague 7, 19, 31
Unfair Contract Terms Act 1977 53, 57, 69
reasonableness 49, 70–1
unfair surprise 72
Unfair Terms in Consumer Contracts Regulations 1999 49, 53, 72
unilateral
contract 8–9
mistake 73
offer 5
unjust enrichment, minors 40

vagueness 7, 19, 31
void contracts 81, 83
common law 40, 101–5
consequences of 106–7
minors 39–40
mistake 81, 83–4
ultra vires 35–7

warranties 49
implied 54–5
'Wednesday' principle 57
withdrawal of offer 3–4, 7–8
written agreement
inclusion of terms 52
performance 88